GUITAR *signature licks*

Mark Knopfler

A step-by-step breakdown of his guitar styles and techniques

by Wolf Marshall

ISBN 0-7935-8129-X

HAL•LEONARD® CORPORATION

7777 W. BLUEMOUND RD. P.O.BOX 13819 MILWAUKEE, WI 53213

Visit Hal Leonard Online at
www.halleonard.com

The Guitar Style of
Mark Knopfler

A MARK KNOPFLER AXOLOGY

GUITARS

Electric guitars: Mark Knopfler's first electric guitar was a red Hofner V-2 Strat copy, acquired in 1965. In the late sixties, he moved on to an early-sixties double-cutaway Gibson Les Paul Special, refinished from black to cherry. By the mid seventies, Mark found his signature sound in the Fender Stratocaster—the famous "Sultans of Swing" Strat heard on most of the early Dire Straits tracks is a vintage 1960 model (serial no. 68354) with a rosewood fingerboard which was refinished (from its original "natural wood" color) in red lacquer. By 1979, Knopfler added a second early-sixties red Strat as a back-up. This one had a maple fingerboard and a DiMarzio pickup in the neck position. In this period, he also occasionally used an old sixties sunburst Telecaster Custom with a rosewood fingerboard and white binding on the body.

During the early eighties, Mark entered his "Schecter period". Fearing for his vintage Fenders, he had several custom guitars made as replacements. These were assembled from Schecter components, generally heavier in weight—built like tanks—and equipped with either Seymour Duncan Strat or Duncan Vintage Strat pickups. The red Schecter Strat (serial no. S8218) had a maple fingerboard without position dots, heavier bridge saddles, and was electronically configured with two controls and three pickup toggle switches instead of the stock three controls and five-way pickup switch of a Fender Strat. It was featured on "Expresso Love" from 1980's *Making Movies* and became Knopfler's workhorse guitar of the era. A sunburst Schecter Strat (serial no. S8001) with a metal pickguard and the same basic specs replaced Mark's favorite, which was stolen. This instrument is heard on "Tunnel of Love," also from *Making Movies.*

In addition to the Strats, Knopfler had a Schecter Telecaster constructed for him in the early eighties. This is described as "a great rhythm guitar and often supplies the 'picking rhythm' that is Mark's trademark" as exemplified on the track "Walk of Life" from *Brothers in Arms.* It is a red Telecaster Custom copy (serial no. S8703) with a rosewood fingerboard (again without position dots), Duncan vintage pickups, matching painted headstock, and white binding on the body. A second black Schecter Tele Custom (serial no. S8421) was employed as a back-up, and for its "heavier sound."

On 1985's *Brothers in Arms,* discerning listeners could detect yet another addition to the Knopfler sonic arsenal. Mark used a mid-eighties Gibson Les Paul Standard vintage reissue (serial no. 90006) for the uncommon nasal tone of the hit track "Money for Nothing." This guitar was re-wired so that the central position of the pickup selector connected the two pickups "out of phase"—the so-called "Peter Green mod" also reputedly used and much favored by Jimmy Page in his Yardbirds and early Led Zeppelin days. This modification is engaged by a push-pull pot which replaces one of the standard guitar tone controls. It was also heard on "Brothers in Arms" and later on "You and Your Friend" from 1991's *On Every Street.*

In the late eighties, Knopfler switched again, this time to custom-made Pensa-Suhr Strats built by luthier John Suhr and close friend Rudy Pensa, owner of Rudy's Music in New York City. Mark's favorite custom solid-body remains the luxurious instrument (serial no. 001) they produced in 1987. It features a one-piece quilted maple carved top on a mahogany body, a twenty-two-fret bound Brazilian rosewood fingerboard, and a fixed Floyd Rose double-locking tremolo system. Electronically, it is fitted with an EMG active pickup system consisting of two SA single-coils and an 85 bridge humbucker with SPC presence control—a switchable mid-range boost mounted as a push-pull pot on the tone knob. This remarkable guitar is heard to good advantage on "Heavy Fuel" and "Planet of New Orleans" from *On Every Street.*

Other notable electrics in the Knopfler stable include a white John Suhr-built Fender Strat look-alike (complete with decals and vintage parts), a black 1986 Pensa-Suhr Strat (serial no. 014, with EMG pickups and a floating Floyd Rose tremolo system), and an unmodified 1986 sunburst Les Paul Standard reissue (serial no. 12849). Additionally, Mark is known to pull out an electric-acoustic guitar once in a while for different tonal colors. These include a blonde 1953 Gibson Super 400 CES with rare Alnico pickup magnets (serial no. A22087), a sunburst 1960 Gibson ES-175 with humbuckers (serial no. 510514), and a red Gretsch "Super Chet" Model 7690 (serial no. 84055) given to him by Chet Atkins.

Acoustic guitars: Mark's earliest acoustic guitars in the sixties were various borrowed instruments used for his solo gigs in British folk clubs. By the late sixties, while in Leeds, he acquired a 1928 National tricone metal-body (nickel-plated steel guitar) from luthier and friend Steve Phillips. This acoustic, much favored by Hawaiian slide guitarists and country blues players like Son House, Blind Boy Fuller, and Bukka White, became a fixture in the Mark Knopfler arsenal and a hallmark of the Dire Straits sound. His main National in the eighties and nineties was a 1936 "Duolian" Style-O steel guitar (serial no. B1844), retro-fitted with an L.R. Baggs bridge transducer. This cherished instrument was pictured on the cover of Dire Straits' *Brothers in Arms* album, introducing the curious acoustic to the public at large and creating a run on resonator guitars in modern and vintage markets. Mark generally keeps it in open G Tuning, and uses a capo at the second or third fret. Other acoustics in the Knopfler arsenal include a Ramirez nylon-string classical guitar (used on "Private Investigations"), Ovation Adamas twelve- and six-strings, an Ovation legend, a Gibson J-45, a Taylor, a 1925 Gibson L-3 archtop with a round soundhole, and several custom-made guitars built by Steve Phillips.

Strings: On his standard-tuned Strats, Teles, and Les Pauls, Mark Knopfler generally uses D'Addario XL-120s. These are an extra-light gauge set (.009–.042). His open-tuned electrics are strung with .010s. On the Super 400 CES (and other acoustic electrics), Mark prefers the heavier D'Addario XL115W set (.011s with a wound third string). He strings his Nationals with D'Addario J-15 bronze extra-light gauge.

AMPS

Mark Knopfler's earliest amps were small home radios which, in his words, gave him "the awesome power of four-and-a-half watts to blow up in the comfort of my own home." With the Café Racers, he played through a 30-watt Selmer Thunderbird amp. In 1992, Mark mentioned using an old Fender Vibrolux for the "Sultans of Swing" record. This was a small tube combo amp made in the fifties and early sixties, and the perfect mate to his 1960 Strat—together they added up to the definitive early Mark Knopfler tone. Though he experimented with numerous amps throughout his career, the Vibrolux remained a mainstay of his recordings; reprised on later tracks such as "Fade to Black" *(On Every Street)* and "Assassin of Love" *(Miracle).* By 1979, he switched again to more powerful Music Man combo amps with two 12-inch speakers, similar to Fender Twin-Reverbs. In the early eighties, Mark began using a two-amp setup on stage. For this, he employed Mesa Boogie Mark II or Mark III amps with Marshall 4x12 cabinets. Later in the eighties, he switched again to Soldano SLO-100 amps (also favored by Eric Clapton, Eddie Van Halen, Steve Lukather, and Vivian Campbell in this period). These are heard on many of the later Dire

Straits tracks such as "Heavy Fuel," "Calling Elvis," "On Every Street," and "Planet of New Orleans" *(On Every Street)*. Currently, his main amps in the studio and on stage are still the Soldanos. They have been modified by Pete Cornish to separate the preamp and power sections. The amps are connected to 4x12 Marshall cabinets with Electro-Voice 12" speakers. In the studio, he augments the Soldanos with a number of old Fender amps.

EFFECTS

Mark Knopfler began recording with a spartan setup, preferring the sound of the guitar straight into the amp with just a touch of echo, and creating most of his tonal effects with his fingers. His effects in the early days of Dire Straits consisted of a Morley volume pedal and an MXR analog delay stomp box. Most of Mark's effects are echoes and this remains true to the present day. By 1984, he added DeltaLab digital delays to upgrade his signal path. Currently, his effects rig includes a T.C. Electronics 2290 delay, an Alesis Quadraverb, a Boss CE300 analog chorus unit, a Zoom 9010, and a rack-mounted Cry Baby wah (in a fixed setting). This group of processors receives the post-preamp mono signal from two Soldano heads and returns the emerging stereo signal to the two Soldano power-amp sections.

MARK KNOPFLER:
A Selected Discography

Dire Straits

Studio albums: *Dire Straits* (1977) Warner Bros. 3266-2; *Communique* (1979) WB 3330-2; *Making Movies* (1980) WB 3480-2; *Love Over Gold* (1982) WB 9 23728-2; *Brothers in Arms* (1985) WB 9 25264-2; *On Every Street* (1991) WB 9 26680-2; *Twisting by the Pool* WB 29800 (EP)

Live albums: *Alchemy: Dire Straits Live* WB 25085 (double album); *Hope and Anchor Front Row Festival* ; *Live at the BBC* ; *On the Night*

Collections: *Money for Nothing* (1988) WB 25794; *Rainbow Warriors* Greenpeace

Mark Knopfler Solo

Mark Knopfler, *Local Hero* WB 23827; *Golden Heart* WB

With others

Bob Dylan: *Slow Train Coming, and Infidels;* Steely Dan: *Gaucho;* Van Morrison: *Beautiful Visions;* Phillip Lynott: *Solo in Soho,* and *The Phillip Lynott Album;* Bryan Ferry: *Boys and Girls;* Kate and Anna McGarrigle: *Love Over and Over;* The Judds: *River of Time;* Notting Hillbillies: *Missing...Presumed Having a Good Time;* David Knopfler: *Release;* John Illsley: *Never Told a Soul;* Chet Atkins: *Stay Tuned, Neck and Neck,* and *Read My Licks;* Jerry Reed: *Sneakin' Around;* Willy DeVille: *Miracles;* Joan Armatrading: *The Shouting Stage;* Randy Newman: *Land of Dreams;* Various artists (with Chuck Jackson): *Adios Amigo;* Various artists (with Waylon Jennings): *notfadeaway: remembering buddy holly*

Film Scores

Local Hero; Cal; Comfort and Joy; The Princess Bride.

MARK KNOPFLER
VITAL STATISTICS

Born: Glasgow, Scotland, August 12, 1949, to a Hungarian emigrant, an architect, and English teacher.

Raised: Newcastle, England. Mark's family relocated in 1955.

Education: Two years of English, at State University of Leeds (1967–1969). Mark worked as a journalist for the Yorkshire Evening Post in Leeds, and also taught English in college. He received an honorary music doctorate from the University of Newcastle-upon-Tyne in 1983.

Earliest musical experiences: Mark was exposed to Celtic music during his early years in native Scotland. He was introduced to rock 'n' roll at about age 9 through his uncle Kingsley who played boogie-woogie piano. He became an avid radio listener and record buyer.

Early musical training: Mark's father, an amateur musician, interested him in violin and piano. He did not study formally as a youth, and is self-taught (by ear) on the guitar.

Earliest musical influences: English skiffle and American rock 'n' roll (late fifties–early sixties). Mark cites the following artists and records: Lonnie Donegan, early Elvis (Scotty Moore or Chet Atkins, guitar), the Everly Brothers (Atkins, guitar), Ricky Nelson (James Burton, guitar; "Hello, Mary Lou"), Duane Eddy ("Because They're Young"), the Fireballs ("Quite a Party" b/w "Gunshot"), Buddy Holly, Jerry Lee Lewis, the Shadows, Ben E. King ("Spanish Harlem"), and Bruce Channel ("Hey Baby").

Earliest equipment: Hofner V-2, a German-made Strat copy acquired at age fifteen 1964) as a gift from Mark's father, it "cost about 50 quid and had to be red." His earliest amps were jerry-rigged radios of no more than four-and-a-half watts.

Early band and rock guitar influences: (Early to mid sixties) British Invasion bands the Beatles ("Please, Please Me"), the Rolling Stones, and the Kinks ("You Really Got Me"), as well as U.S. groups like the Doors.

Later influences: (Mid to late sixties) Bob Dylan *(Blonde on Blonde)*; American blues guitar—particular favorites included early blues guitarists Blind Willie McTell, Blind Blake, and Lonnie Johnson, Chicago blues singer Howlin' Wolf, and guitarist B.B.King (particularly the *Live at the Regal* record), Head, Hands, and Feet (with Albert Lee on guitar), and J.J. Cale.

Other influences: Italian "spaghetti western" film composer Ennio Morricone. Traditional Irish music and western swing.

Early bands: In Northern England—Brewer's Droop, an R&B/Cajun group. In London—The Café Racers, a rockabilly/R&B band, just prior to Dire Straits (mid seventies). It was at this time that Mark developed his fingerstyle technique.

Principal band: Dire Straits, formed in the summer of 1977. Original personnel—Mark Knopfler (vocals, lead & rhythm guitars), David Knopfler (rhythm guitar), John Illsley (bass), Pick Withers (drums).

Recording sessions: Dire Straits, Steely Dan, Bob Dylan, Van Morrison, Bryan Ferry, Aztec Camera, Phil Everly, Randy Newman, Joan Armatrading, Phil Lynott, Ben E. King, Chet Atkins, Jerry Reed, Willy de Ville, The Judds, Jeff Healey, Ronnie Milsap, Waylon Jennings, American Red Cross Gulf Crisis Fund, and many others.

Awards: BRIT Award: Best British Group—Dire Straits (1983); Ivor Novello Award: Outstanding British Lyric—"Private Investigations" (1983); Ivor Novello Award: Best Film or Theme Song—"Going Home" (1984); Silver Clef: Outstanding Services to British Music—Dire Straits (1985). BRIT Award: Best British Group—Dire Straits (1986); Grammy: Best Rock Performance—"Money for Nothing" (1986); Grammy: Best Engineered Record (Non-Classical)—*Brothers in Arms* (1986); Grammy: Best Country Instrumental Performance—"Cosmic Square Dance" (with Chet Atkins); MTV Award: Best Video and Best Group Video—"Money for Nothing" (1986); BRIT Award: Best British Album—*Brothers in Arms* (1987) Grammy: Best Music Video, Long Form category—*Dire Straits Brothers in Arms* (1987); Ivor Novello award: Outstanding Contribution to British Music (1989); Grammy: Best Country Vocal Collaboration—"Poor Boy Blues" (1991); Grammy: Best Country Instrumental Performance—"So Soft, Your Goodbye" (with Chet Atkins) (1991)

The songs in this volume came from the following records (all on Warner Brothers).

Dire Straits (1978): "Sultans of Swing"
Communiqué (1979): "Once Upon a Time in the West"
Making Movies (1980): "Tunnel of Love," "Expresso Love"
Love Over Gold (1982): "Telegraph Road," "Private Investigations," "Love Over Gold"
Brothers in Arms (1985): "Money for Nothing," "Walk of Life," "Brothers in Arms"
On Every Street (1991): "You and Your Friend," "Heavy Fuel," "Planet of New Orleans"

THE RECORDING

Wolf Marshall: guitars
Mike Sandberg: drums and percussion
Michael Della Gala: bass
John Nau: keyboards

Glenn Nishida: audio engineer (drums and percussion). Pacifica Studios, Los Angeles, CA
Wolf Marshall: audio engineer (overdubs and mixdown). Marshall Arts Studio, Malibu, CA
Brent Backhus: editor. Digitally edited at Reel Time, Los Angeles, CA

Produced by Wolf Marshall

Special thanks to Soldano amps, Jimmy Dunlop at Dunlop Manufacturing, and Del Breckenfeld, artists relations, Fender Musical Instruments.
Special thanks to Soldano amps for the skinny on "Money for Nothing."
Extra special thanks to Marie Noerdlinger, Don Young, and McGregor Gaines at National Reso-Phonic Guitars for the gorgeous National Style-O used on "Telegraph Road" and "You and Your Friend."

SULTANS OF SWING (Dire Straits – 1978)

Words and Music by Mark Knopfler

Fig. 1 – Intro, Verses

Dire Straits was formed in London in the summer of 1977. In less than two years, the band achieved platinum status and international pop acclaim with their debut album *Dire Straits* and the single "Sultans of Swing." One of rock's favorite rags-to-riches stories, Dire Straits came about when vocalist-guitarist-composer Mark Knopfler got together with his brother David (rhythm guitar), bassist John Illsley, and drummer Pick Withers to record a demo of "Sultans of Swing" for the sum of $180. BBC disc jockey Charlie Gillett took a liking to the song, and put it into the Radio London playlist, where it created a groundswell of public reaction prompting the British label Phonograph to offer the group a record contract to do it right. The rest is history.

"Sultans of Swing" was Dire Straits' first big hit. The song broke the British Top 10 and was a standout track on the first album. It was #4 on the U.S. Billboard charts in February, 1979, and remained in the Top 40 for twelve weeks. Consisting of deceptively simple ingredients, "Sultans of Swing" is a definitive early Mark Knopfler outing, distinguished by his husky vocals and unmistakable guitar sound. Interestingly, Knopfler wrote the song on his National acoustic, open-tuned, but it came alive and evolved into the hit we know and love when he played the same parts on his Strat plugged into an old Vibrolux.

"Sultans of Swing" is a perfect vehicle for Mark Knopfler's unique style and features his signature electric guitar tone prominently in the mix. Noted for exerting enormous influence on both sides of the Atlantic, the clean Strat timbre, played with Knopfler's inimitable fingerstyle approach (emanating from an old Fender tube amp), was almost immediately acknowledged and revered as the "Mark Knopfler sound."

The "Mark Knopfler sound" revolves around two key concepts. The first is mechanical and involves the guitar itself. Initially, Mark achieved his trademark glassy tone by using the "in between" (so-called "out-of-phase") position of the selector switch to combine the bridge and middle pickups. In the days of the first two Dire Straits records, he taped his stock three-position Strat pickup switch to notch a pre-set position, but by the third album was using a retro-fitted, five-position switch for the purpose. Taken for granted nowadays as a primary tonal color of the electric guitar, the sound was largely pioneered and popularized by Knopfler in the late seventies.

The second aspect of Mark's sound is purely physical. Prior to the formation of Dire Straits, he realized that "the best amplifiers are picks," and accordingly developed a fingerstyle technique using the thumb and (mainly) first two fingers to articulate chords and melodies rather than relying on a conventional plectrum. This led to the creation of a highly personal and identifiable sound in which subtle dynamics could be emphasized for extremely musical and soulful results—heard on record throughout his career. He follows no specific, regimented pattern of picking, instead favoring an intuitive approach determined by the melody and the phrase itself.

In "Sultans of Swing," both of these signature components are at the forefront. The main guitar sound (Gtr.1) is the Strat processed with a touch of echo—Knopfler's effect of choice—which enhances both chords and single notes. Mark's snappy rhythm work in the intro and verse provides a few beautiful examples of his pianistic chord-plucking technique. This is heard throughout the song, particularly in the comping of the verse (in measures 2–3, 20, and 43–53). The last four measures of the second verse (51–54) establish a thematic main riff of triads (Dm/A, C/G, B♭/F, and F/A) which is central to the tune, appearing between verses and at the end of the solo. The tasty, understated single-note fills in the intro and verses present another example of Knopfler's fingerstyle technique in action. These sparse but memorable gems hint at a gamut of remolded influences from swing-based, jazz-oriented lines to blues and country licks. Notable points include the predominate use of arpeggios (measures 4–7 and 23–24), intervallic lines (measures 15–16), and the inclusion of the ninth (E in D minor, as in measure 7) in the melodies. Behind the intro and verses, and throughout "Sultans of Swing," a buoyant two-guitar groove, typical of early Dire Straits, propels things along nicely with a combination of straight eighth-note strumming, flamenco-inspired *rasqueado* flourishes (sometimes also called "frailing"), choke-muted percussive textures, and syncopated rhythms.

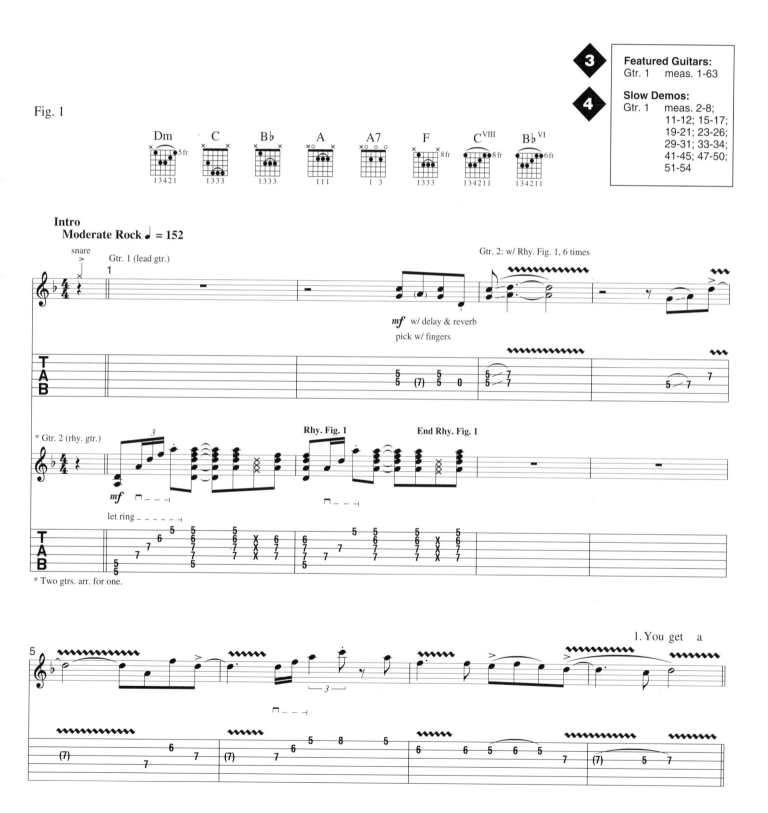

Fig. 1

3 Featured Guitars:
Gtr. 1   meas. 1-63

4 Slow Demos:
Gtr. 1   meas. 2-8;
           11-12; 15-17;
           19-21; 23-26;
           29-31; 33-34;
           41-45; 47-50;
           51-54

Fig. 2 – Guitar Solo 1

The soloing in "Sultans of Swing" is definitive Knopfler. In the internal solo (3:27–4:13) and in the outro solo (4:58 to fade-out), it is possible to find most of the signature elements of his lead style—arpeggios, unusual diatonic melodies, chromaticism, and mutated blues and country licks. Mark's use of arpeggios is exemplary. He frequently plays off the chord shapes of the backing changes to create interesting lines. We hear this approach in the first solo in measures 3–5 (arpeggios outlining A major and D minor) and in measures 16–19 (Bb and C arpeggios). Blues-oriented bends are found in measures 1 and 15. The quasi-pedal-steel bends in measures 9 and 10 are another sonic trademark. For these types of country-inflected lines, Knopfler uses an oblique bend to produce the crying effect. In measure 9, he bends a G to an A on the third string while fretting F and C above on the first and second strings—outlining an F triad in the process. A typical variation of this lick is found in measure 20, where it acts as a transition back to the main rhythm riff and the sixth verse.

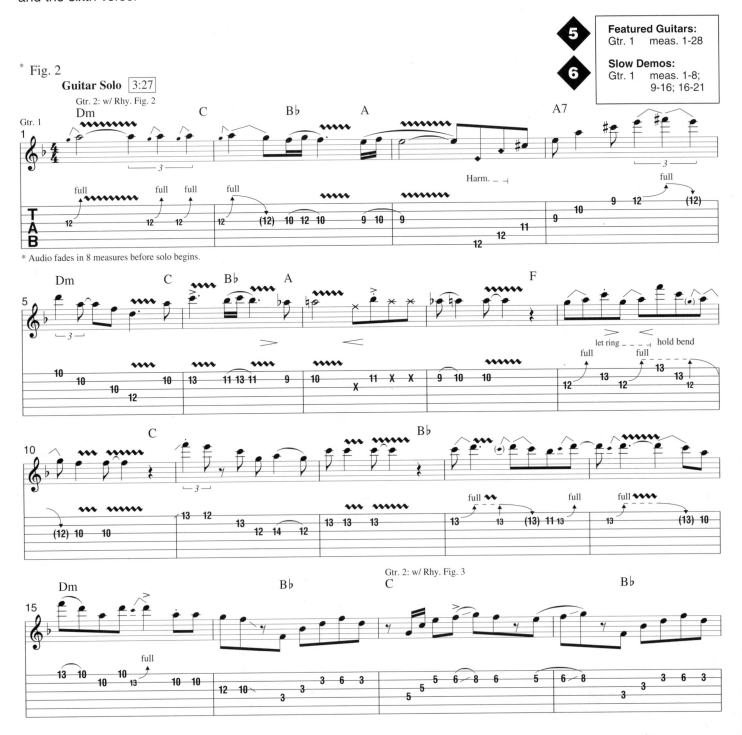

Featured Guitars:
Gtr. 1   meas. 1-28

Slow Demos:
Gtr. 1   meas. 1-8;
          9-16; 16-21

* Audio fades in 8 measures before solo begins.

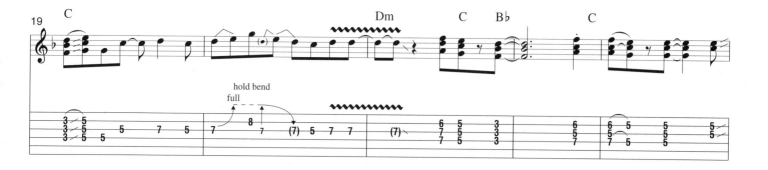

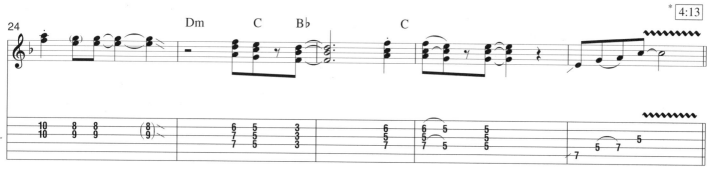

* Track 5 continues on, 8 more measures before fading out.

Fig.3 – Outro Solo

Mark stretches out and elaborates in his outro solo (4:58–5:46). He balances eclectic melodic ideas, slick phrasing, florid improvisation, and tight structure in a very musical way—so much so that this compositional approach to improvised solos would become a hallmark of his style. Here are a few of the most noteworthy points: Knopfler begins with a well-placed blues line in D minor pentatonic. This is complemented by a slippery, descending legato line in C major pentatonic (measures 3–4), which is answered by a rolling country guitar ostinato riff (measures 7–8). Note the legato hammer-on/pull-off phrasing. In measures 9–10 (5:11), we find Mark personalizing a Chicago blues cliché. Check out the atypical interval jump and characteristic arpeggio outline worked into the lick. In measures 13–17, a classic Knopfler phrase is heard. Representing a real climax in the solo, it is made of rapid-fire sixteenth-note pull-offs. These are arranged as triad arpeggios on the first and second strings, and played as a furious ostinato sequence spelling out the chord progression of Dm–Bb–C. Note the common tones (F and D) linking the first two shapes together and the common physical shapes of the Bb and C major in the phrase—further evidence of Mark's melodic-harmonic savvy translated to the guitar.

Featured Guitars:
Gtr. 1   meas. 1-25

Slow Demos:
Gtr. 1   meas. 1-8;
9-12; 13-16;
18-21

* Audio fades in 8 measures before solo begins.

ONCE UPON A TIME IN THE WEST
(Communiqué – 1979)

Words and Music by Mark Knopfler

Fig.4 – Intro Solo

"Once upon a Time in the West," a leading track from Dire Straits' sophomore effort *(Communiqué),* was reputedly written by Mark Knopfler in an inebriated condition—in his own words, "while watching the film in altered state." It is distinguished by a moody free-time intro which showcases Mark's early penchant for guitar orchestrating. The lead instrument (Gtr. 1) plays trills and slinky solo lines against a light two-guitar backing, while Gtr. 2 rubs the strings with the palm in a tremolo style for an interesting textural effect and plays higher partial-chord voicings. A simpler, supportive barre-chord part made of lower-register voicings is played by Gtr. 3. The band comes in at 0:26, where the tempo and basic feel are also established. Check out the blend of influences in the funk-meets-reg-gae opening (main) groove, made more intriguing with its three interlocking guitar parts. Note also the fluctuating 4/4 and 3/4 measures used to accommodate the odd phrase lengths. Here, the backing guitars are again orchestral and well-arranged—Gtr. 2 is a funky chordal part, while Gtr. 3 plays lower, fuller voicings with occasional embellishments and various muted and choked textures. On top, Mark adds well-placed trademark lead lines. The two-string bends in measures 11–12 and 16–17 are well-known Knopfler signatures. They are also thematic elements recalled elsewhere in the song. The first is a dyad of D and F♯ (D major) on the third and second strings bent to E and G. The second is a D and F dyad (D minor) bent up to E and G. Both have a slick quasi-steel guitar sound near and dear to Knopfler's heart.

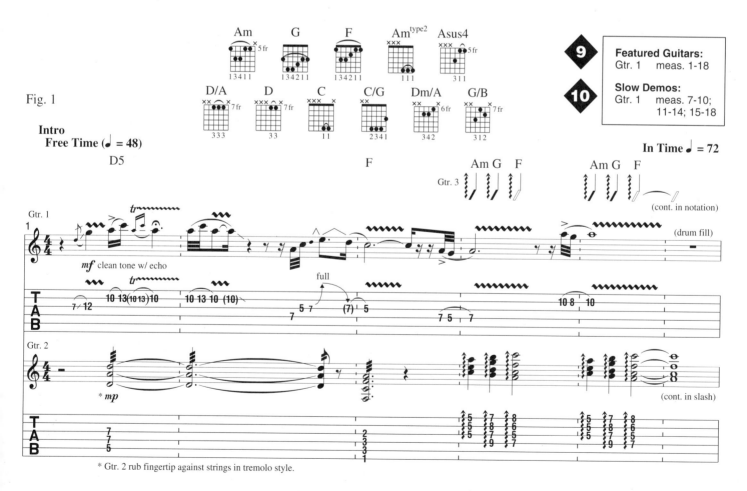

Featured Guitars:
Gtr. 1   meas. 1-18

Slow Demos:
Gtr. 1   meas. 7-10;
              11-14; 15-18

* "choke". Staccato mute by lifting your fingers off the fretboard immediately after striking chord.

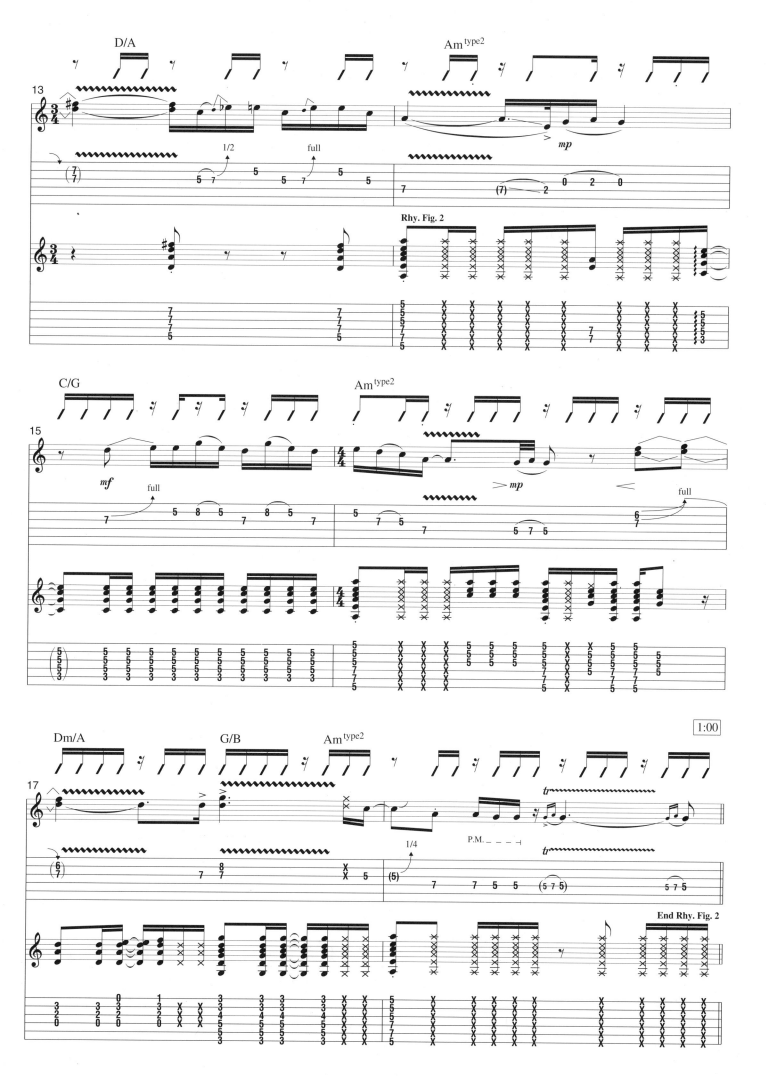

Fig.5 – Guitar Solo

Begun at 2:09, Mark's tuneful excursion is a study in soloing over *mixed meters.* Note the 4/4, 3/4, and 2/4 measures in addition to the various chord changes in the section. In characteristic Knopfler fashion, he flawlessly negotiates each change of rhythm and harmony while maintaining a smooth melodic flow and the highest degree of soul—brought to the fore with his unmistakable fingerpicked, dynamic-conscious touch. The chord progression indicates a combination of A Dorian (emphasized by the D major chord) and A Aeolian (natural minor) modes, both staples of the Mark Knopfler soloing and songwriting style. His solo melodies reflect these background changes, often incorporating the operative chord tones of the progression. Check out the F♯ in the tasty but uncommon bent-string lick in measure 11. Classic Knopfler lines can be found in the bluesy pull-offs (used against modal chord changes) of measures 1–2, the arpeggios (often characteristically raked) in measures 9, 13, and 15, and the country-inflected bends of measures 4, 11, and 20.

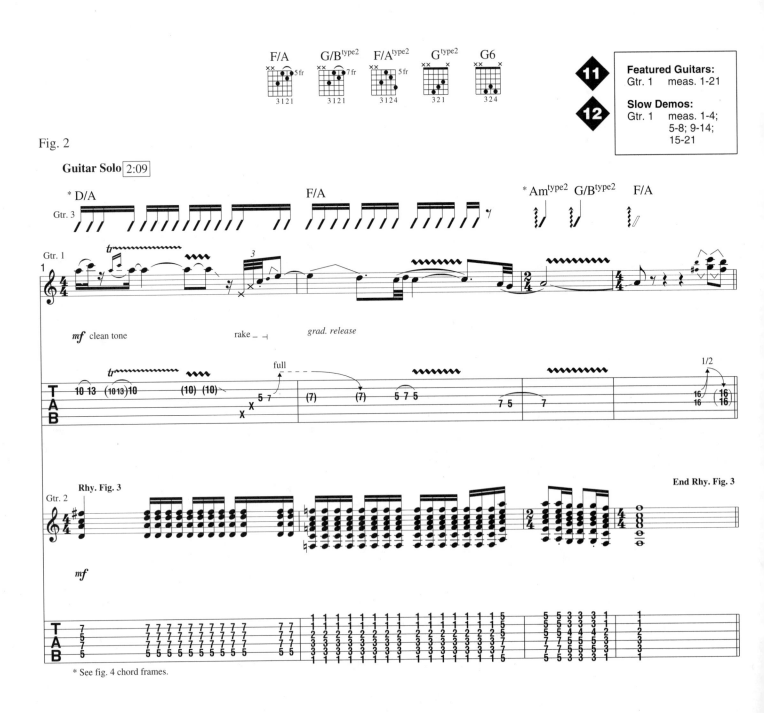

Featured Guitars:
Gtr. 1   meas. 1-21

Slow Demos:
Gtr. 1   meas. 1-4;
         5-8; 9-14;
         15-21

* See fig. 4 chord frames.

Half-Time Feel 2:21

Gtr. 2: w/ Rhy. Fig. 1, simile

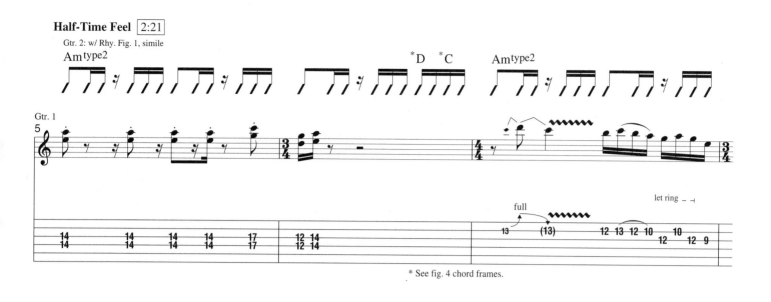

* See fig. 4 chord frames.

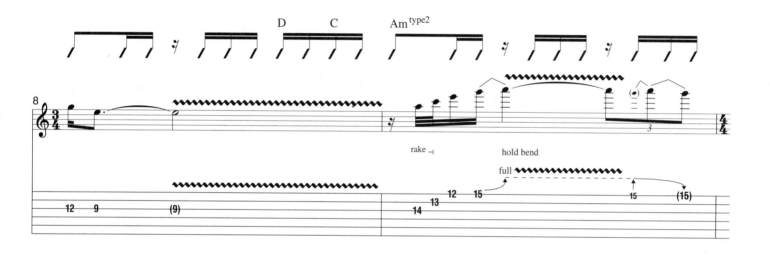

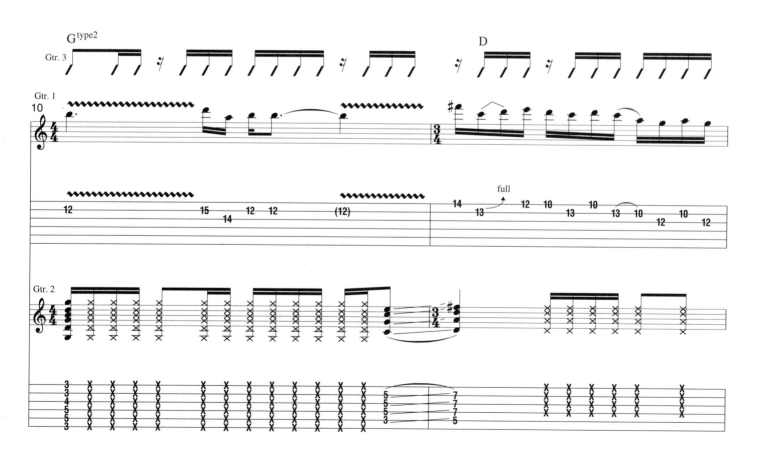

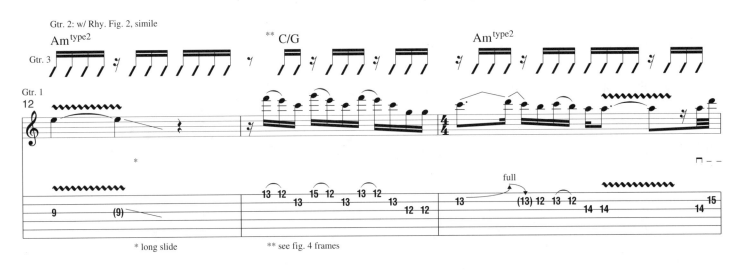

* long slide   ** see fig. 4 frames

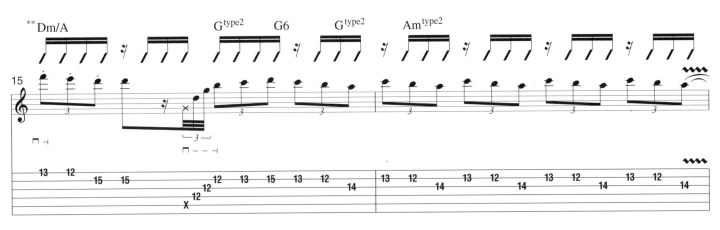

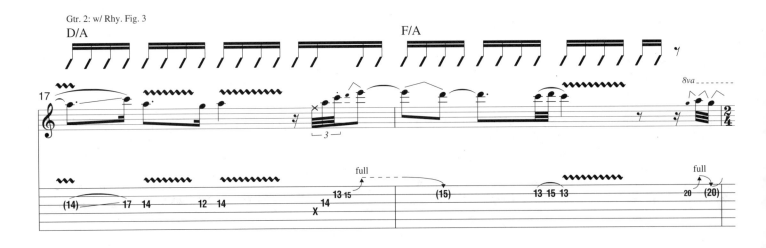

3:06

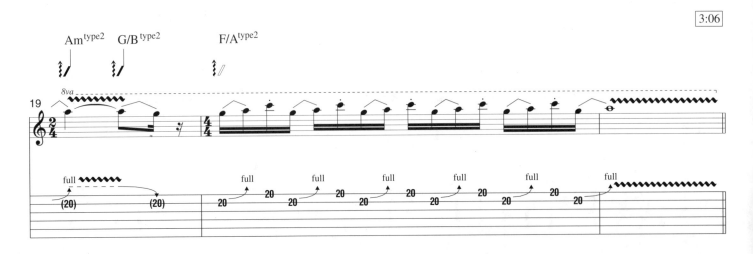

TUNNEL OF LOVE
(Making Movies – 1980)

Words and Music by Mark Knopfler

Fig. 1 – Outro Solo

The outro solo in "Tunnel of Love" is a classic Mark Knopfler moment. In his preferred key of F major (or D minor), he takes the entire coda section—almost two minutes long—to build an extended 57-measure solo teeming with musical signatures. The solo proceeds compositionally, with Mark introducing and developing motives—the light, singable diatonic melodies of the first eighteen measures (5:57–6:25)—over an ethereal, fingerpicked rhythm guitar (Gtr. 2). Notice the variety of dynamics in this section. Mark shapes each statement with care, often varying his attack to go from a purr to a growl within the same phrase. The arrangement begins to build at 6:26. Here, another guitar enters (Gtr.3, a steel-string acoustic), and Mark plays with more intensity and volume—favoring an edge-of-distortion tone emphasized by heavier fingerpicked attacks and occasional pulled-and-snapped string accents. In measures 19–26, he elaborates on the solo's opening themes, delivering a series of gutsy lines which gather momentum toward the first climax (6:40). This climax section features a country-inspired oblique string-bend lick leading to a serpentine scalar passage slurring elegantly down the G string (measures 27–28). The country influence is also heard in the ensuing slurred-sixth double stops found in measures 31–33. The pull-off arpeggio flurries (outlining F–Fsus4–F chords melodically on the first two strings) in measures 49–50 are an unmistakable Knopfler trademark, as are the D minor lines which follow. In those D minor licks of measures 51–54, notice the familiar melodic inclusion of the ninth (E) into the Dm chord sound—a mainstay of the Knopfler single-note approach.

Featured Guitars:
Gtr. 1   meas. 1-55

Slow Demos:
Gtr. 1   meas. 1-10;
          11-18; 19-27;
          27-32; 32-41;
          41-49; 49-57

Fig. 1

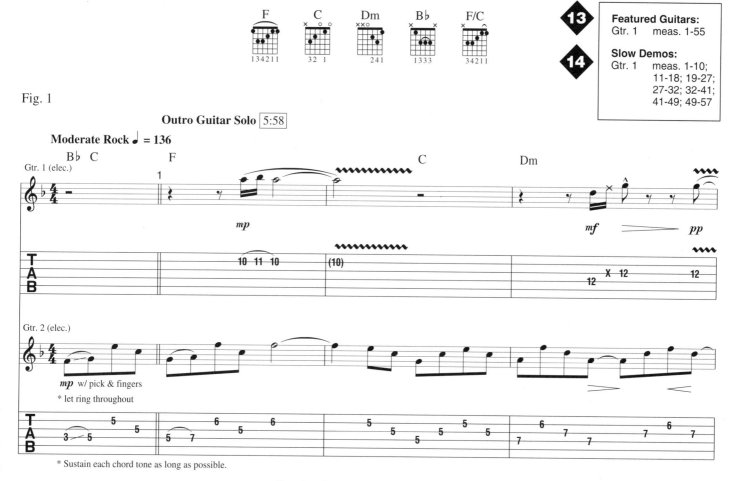

Outro Guitar Solo 5:58

Moderate Rock ♩ = 136

* let ring throughout

* Sustain each chord tone as long as possible.

** Strum lightly w/ fingertip.

* Strum lightly w/ fingertip.

* Strum lightly w/ fingertip

* Strum lightly w/ fingertip. ** Louder w/ slight distortion on accents.

** Gtr. volume up for drive.

EXPRESSO LOVE
(Making Movies – 1980)

Words and Music by Mark Knopfler

Fig. 1 – Intro, Verse, and Chorus

Dire Straits entered the eighties with some significant changes. Rhythm guitarist David Knopfler left to pursue a solo career and the band carried on as a quartet. The music was also evolving toward greater finesse and complexity, as evidenced by 1980's *Making Movies*. Compared with the first two albums, *Making Movies* was a more sprawling and ambitious work. Worthy of the cinematic connotations of its title, it was distinguished by greater attention to orchestration and recording techniques, more sophisticated, larger-scale arrangements, and the power-pop production acumen of co-producer Jimmy Iovine. The departure of David Knopfler prompted Mark to explore more elaborate keyboard textures—provided by Roy Bittan of the E-Street band—on this record. With its layered arrangement, keyboard touches, and eclectic tangents, "Expresso Love" is a perfect example of the next incarnation of Dire Straits.

     "Expresso Love" is also one of those rare instances where Mark Knopfler played with a pick. He generally favors a flat pick for pure strumming parts on both electric and acoustic, and this song's intro is a case in point. It is comprised of a single D5 power chord which defines the rhythm feel with its well-accented, rumba-based groove. Note that the upper two notes of the chord are often sustained while the chunky eighth-note pulse continues below on the fifth string. In measures 5–12 (0:12), the main riff is introduced. This is a heavier power chord rhythm figure using root-fifth voicings with bass-register passing tones woven through the changes. The riff implies D natural minor (the Aeolian mode)—one of Mark's favorite keys—with the chords D5–Bb5–G5–C5, and is used in the verses as Rhy. Fig. 1 from 0:26–0:53. In the last eight measures of the verse, Knopfler embellishes the section with a colorful overdubbed rhythm part (Rhy. Fig. 2, on Gtr. 2) consisting of triads, dyads, and muted string scrapes. This is a signature chord phrase employing shapes and articulations similar to the "Sultans of Swing" rhythm part. The chorus at 0:53 features a half-time rhythm feel. Notice more interaction between the two guitars, as their established roles (Gtr. 1: rhythm, Gtr. 2: color) are further exploited at this point of the arrangement. The tone on this track exemplifies Knopfler's early eighties sound: a semi-clean custom Schecter Strat (usually with echo) played through a Mesa-Boogie head with a Marshall cabinet.

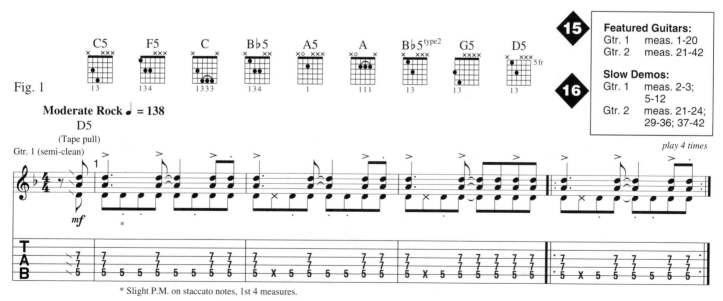

Fig. 1

Moderate Rock ♩ = 138

* Slight P.M. on staccato notes, 1st 4 measures.

Featured Guitars:
Gtr. 1   meas. 1-20
Gtr. 2   meas. 21-42

Slow Demos:
Gtr. 1   meas. 2-3;
            5-12
Gtr. 2   meas. 21-24;
            29-36; 37-42

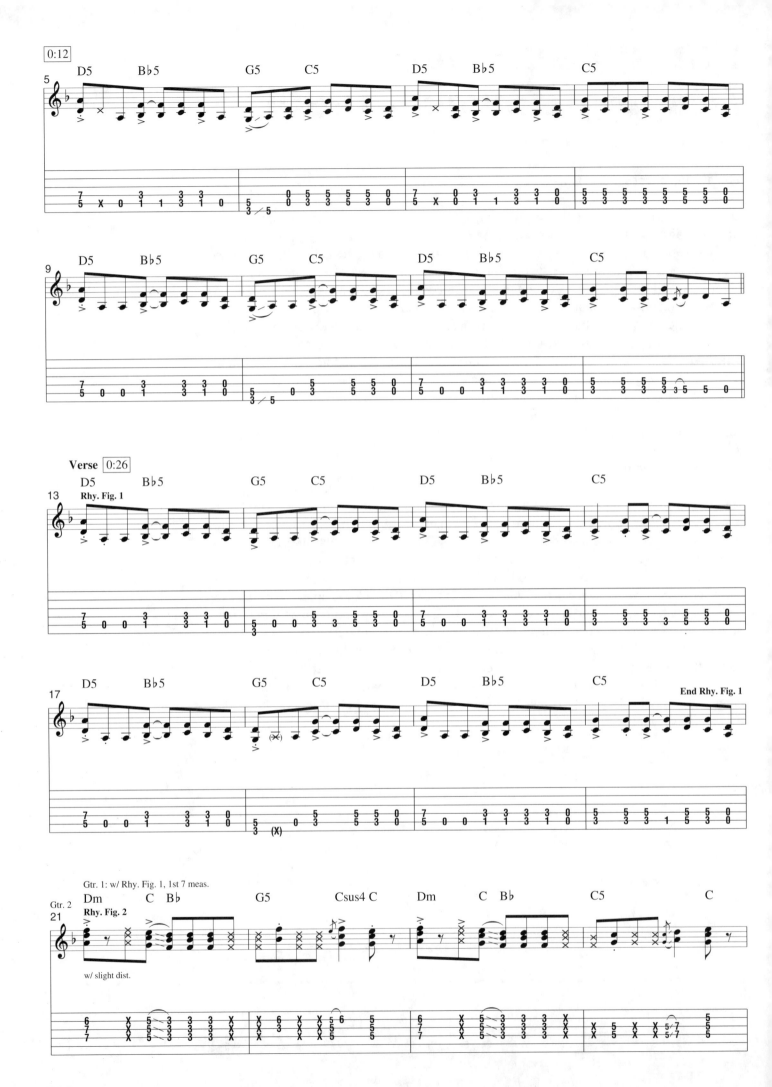

Fig. 2 – Guitar Solo

The guitar solo at 2:27 is a well-conceived outing featuring dual guitar *counterpoint*—something of a rarity in the Mark Knopfler solo catalog at this point. Mark begins his solo on Gtr. 3 with simple, singable diatonic lines reflecting the backing D minor chords. The harmony commences at 2:40. This is an eight-measure section constructed in two tight four-measure phrases. Notice Knopfler's thoughtful but uncommon handling of the dual guitars. The rhythm is virtually identical in both parts (Gtr. 3 and Gtr. 4). This type of counterpoint is referred to as note-against-note, or *first species*. Check out the independent melodies of the two guitars throughout. This is particularly evident in measures 9, 11, 13, and 15, where there is a great deal of contrary motion. In measures 10, 12, 14, and 16, the guitars play more parallel melodies using fourths and fifths as the predominate intervals—all in all, a unique and striking Dire Straits guitar moment.

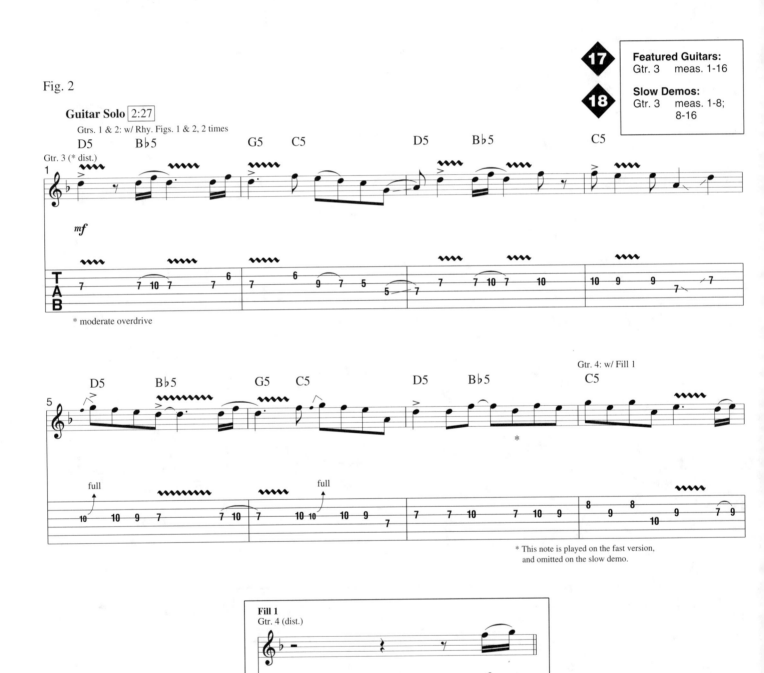

TELEGRAPH ROAD
(Love Over Gold – 1982)

Words and Music by Mark Knopfler

Fig. 1 – Guitar Solo

With *Love Over Gold,* Dire Straits presented their most elaborate album to date. Mark Knopfler was the sole producer of the record and concentrated heavily on textures, orchestration, and overdubs. This 1982 release featured a five-piece Dire Straits lineup comprised of three original members: Knopfler, guitars and vocals; John Illsley, bass; and Pick Withers, drums; with newcomers Alan Clark, keyboards; and Hal Lindes, second guitar. Ed Walsh was called in for additional synth programming, and Mike Mainieri (vibes and marimba), augmented the sound on a couple of tracks. A well-crafted though grandiose work, *Love Over Gold* was a musical milestone for Dire Straits and offered such future classics as the title track, "Private Investigations," and "Telegraph Road."

Mark Knopfler's famed National reso-phonic brass-bodied acoustic (Gtr. 1) is heard prominently on "Telegraph Road." This is a single-resonator model noted for its quick response and edgy metallic sound. Here it adds an atmospheric bluesy touch—its forté—to the track. The National is tuned to open G, a favored slack tuning among country-blues guitarists. This is accomplished by lowering the sixth, fifth, and first strings a whole step each, creating the alternate pitches (from low to high) D–G–D–G–B–D, essentially an open G chord. On this track, Mark capo'd the National at the third fret to transpose the open G-tuned notes to B flat (from low to high: F–Bb–F–Bb–D–F), a preferred key center closer to F major and D minor. It is used to play the ringing arpeggiated chord figures heard in the solo and the verses. In addition to the acoustic, Knopfler overdubbed a distorted electric rhythm part (Gtr. 2) made largely of power chords to further augment and color the guitar orchestration.

Mark plays a light, understated electric solo over this orchestral texture at 4:08. Showcasing his signature clean Strat tone (Gtr. 3), the solo is distinguished by numerous familiar musical traits including melodic scalar lines (connoting at various points either F major or D minor), silky string bends, occasional chord partials, and arpeggio outlines. Note that he favors F major pentatonic (F–G–A–C–D) for the closing lines in the last six measures of the solo. The tag lick at 4:42 emphasizes the new chords of Dm–F/D–G–D with operative tones (B and F♯) skillfully worked into the melodies. The slippery double-timed line of the tag is a particularly noteworthy Knopfler moment—one where he seamlessly blends technique with melodicism.

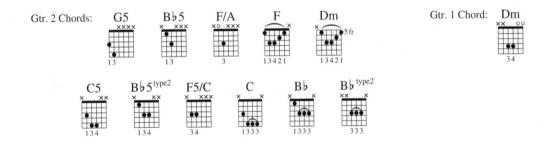

Fig. 1

* Symbols in parentheses represent chord names respective to capo'd guitars. Symbols above reflect actual sounding chords.
** Omitted on slow demo.

* Chords implied by keyboard & bass.

Fig. 2 – Outro Guitar Solo

The mood is darker and more melancholy in Mark's second solo (5:50). The tempo in this section is slower (quarter note = 76 bpm) with minimal accompaniment, leaving plenty of room for Knopfler's soulful and spacious guitar passages. Here his tone (on Gtr. 3) is also a shade dirtier—with more gain but still very "Stratty". Points of interest include the blend of the D harmonic minor scale (D–E–F–G–A–B♭–C♯) and the Aeolian mode (D–E–F–G–A–B♭–C). Notice that he sneaks in a tasty, momentum-gathering D blues lick in the eighth measure to lead into the second chorus (6:15). The Django-inspired lick in measure 10 is another highlight. Check out the signature raked arpeggio—in this case, G diminished over the backing A7♯5 chord—as well as the provocative D harmonic minor/chromatic descending line which follows. These generate a sophisticated jazz-oriented sound. Knopfler plays with intervallic ideas in measures 11–14. Here we find tritone (flat five) and fourth leaps in the melody mixed with more conventional scalar lines. The closing line is a majestic climbing phrase in two-guitar parallel-thirds harmony. The final note is swelled in with the volume control. Knopfler uses a volume pedal as opposed to his guitar knob for these types of effects.

Fig. 2

Outro Guitar Solo 5:50

Moderately Slow Rock ♩ = 76

Featured Guitars:
Gtr. 3   meas. 1-17

Slow Demos:
Gtr. 3   meas. 1-10;
          10-17

* lower volume on gtr.

** Chords implied by keyboard, bass & gtr. combined.

37

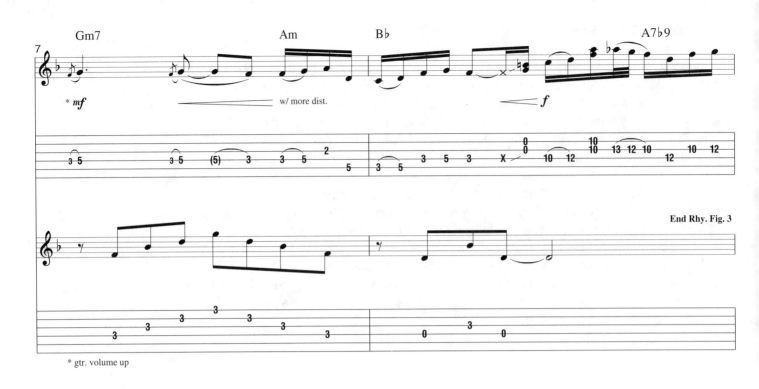

* gtr. volume up

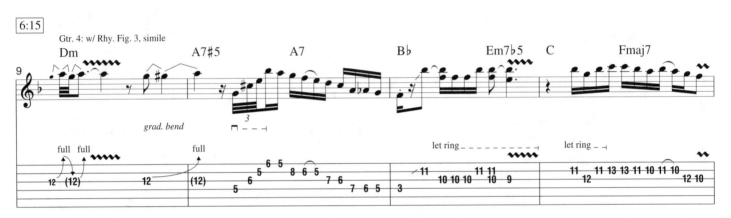

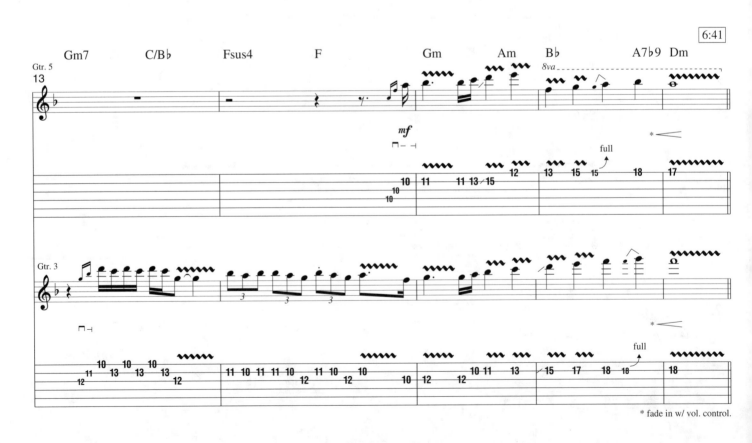

* fade in w/ vol. control.

PRIVATE INVESTIGATIONS
(Love Over Gold – 1982)

Words and Music by Mark Knopfler

Fig. 1 – Guitar Solo 1

"Private Investigations" flaunts the Ennio Morricone (Italian movie soundtrack composer) influence—what Mark Knopfler calls his "spaghetti music"—captured in the song's dramatic arrangement. In his first solo (3:01), Mark reacts to the atmosphere with an airy sound and a semi-classical direction on nylon-string acoustic guitar (Gtr. 1) over a rich but subdued orchestral texture. His statements are tight, well-conceived, and organized into clear phrases which allude to the background progression. Notice the purposeful outlining of each chord with specific melody lines in measures 5–10. Mark's arpeggio approach figures prominently in this section. The G and F changes each receive distinctive broken-chord melodies, with a particularly angular line in measure 6. This passage is a little tricky and requires some extra agility. It slurs out of and back into position quickly within the continuous sixteenth-note rhythm of the line. In measure 7, Knopfler employs a jazz-based procedure when he ascends with an A diminished arpeggio (A–C–D♯–F♯) and descends using the compatible E harmonic minor scale (E–F♯–G–A–B–C–D♯) against B/F♯. Arpeggios are also a significant factor in measures 8–10. Check out the ninth (F♯) added to the E minor arpeggio in measure 8, the straight G diminished arpeggio melody in measure 9, and the Am9 outline in measure 10. The use of Am9 over F♯m7♭5 is another familiar jazz-oriented sound and a staple of Mark Knopfler's improvisational style.

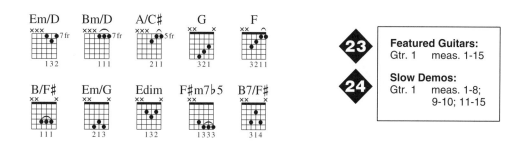

Featured Guitars:
Gtr. 1   meas. 1-15

Slow Demos:
Gtr. 1   meas. 1-8;
          9-10; 11-15

Fig. 1

Fig. 2 – Solo 2

Mark's second solo is played over an E minor background—consisting of a throbbing bass pedal and sparse vibe/marimba licks. It is a brooding, atmospheric moment which epitomizes the Morricone influence. His lines are primarily in E natural minor (Aeolian mode: E–F#–G–A–B–C–D)—which suits the spacious, haunting mood of the section admirably. Notice the overt use of arpeggios (the ascending E minor chordal outline in measure 1 is unmistakable) and the added ninth (F#) to the melodies. The E blues scale (E–G–A–B♭–B–D) and a blues feeling is suggested in the imitative phrases of measures 8 and 11, with the flat fifth tone (B♭) and the call-and-response phrase structure. Mark's famous "snap" plucking adds a strong dynamic element to measure 10. He produces this sound by pulling the string away from the fretboard and then releasing it, letting it ricochet and snap against the surface for a forceful, percussive effect.

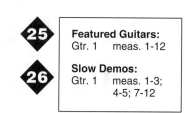

Fig. 2

Guitar Solo 4:04

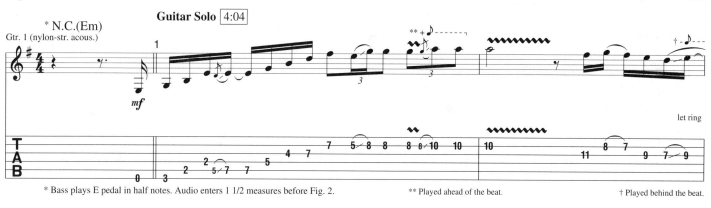

* Bass plays E pedal in half notes. Audio enters 1 1/2 measures before Fig. 2.   ** Played ahead of the beat.   † Played behind the beat.

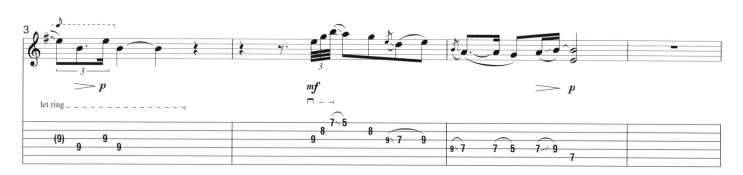

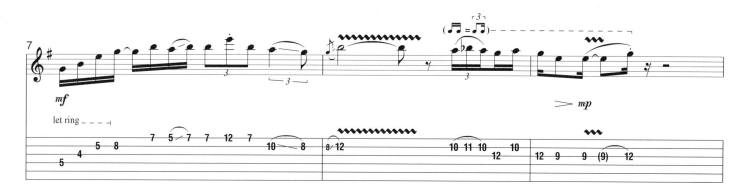

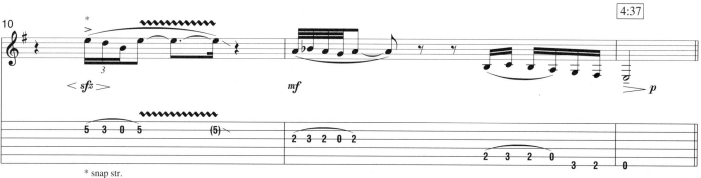

* snap str.

LOVE OVER GOLD
(Love Over Gold – 1982)

Words and Music by Mark Knopfler

Fig. 1 – Intro

"Love Over Gold" begins by presenting the song's main theme in a delicate intro. In its initial form, the theme is stated lightly—almost tentatively—as a sort of concerto-style duet with acoustic piano and nylon-string acoustic guitar (Gtr. 1). Mark's melody is highly emotional, filled with dynamics and nuance. It is built from a characteristic blend of arpeggios and diatonic scalar melody. Note the expressive slides and legato ornaments in the first twelve measures. These are offset nicely by the funkier slurred double stops and chord partials in measures 13–16.

27 Featured Guitars:
Gtr. 1   meas. 1-17

28 Slow Demos:
Gtr. 1   meas. 1-17

Fig. 1

* Chords implied by gtr. & kybd.

Fig. 2 – Interlude

A gorgeous textural interlude is created at 3:13. The music is distinguished by a sonic tapestry of overlapping guitars in staggered entrances and some simple but intriguing layered counterpoint. It centers on a dialog between three guitars: two clean electrics and one nylon-string acoustic. The primary voice (Gtr. 1) plays the lead melodies, essentially further developments of the main theme heard in the intro. An electric guitar processed with echo and chorus (Gtr. 2) supports this main melody with doubled lines in measures 9–14, light counterpoint (including some vocalesque volume-pedal swelled lines) in measures 1–8, and tasteful incidental fills. Another accompaniment part on electric (Gtr. 3), also with echo, consists of arpeggiated chords (measures 1–12) and strummed whole-note chords (measures 13–16).

* swell w/ vol. control

* Slow demo plays A instead of B♭.

MONEY FOR NOTHING
(Brothers in Arms – 1985)

Words and Music by Mark Knopfler & Sting

Fig. 1 – Intro, Verse, and Chorus

"Money for Nothing" was a huge mid-eighties pop-rock hit which establish-ed and cement-ed the MTV era (with the recurring slogan "I Want My MTV"). The song held the #1 posi-tion on the charts for three weeks in the summer of 1985 and, for many, summed up the sentiments of the period. A stand-out piece from the stand-out *Brothers in Arms* album (their biggest seller yet), "Money for Nothing" sported a new Dire Straits lineup. In addition to the core members: Mark Knopfler, John Illsley, and Alan Clark, the group also included the talents of Guy Fletcher (keyboards and vocals) and Terry Williams (or Omar Hakim) on drums, as well as featured guest vocalist and collaborator Sting.

Knopfler's electric guitar enters at 1:36—after a lavish orchestral opening consist-ing of thick synth pads enveloping Sting's unmistakable falsetto wails. The sound here is atypical—distorted, honky and biting. Setting aside his trademark clean Strat and Fender amp setup, Mark employed a modified Les Paul plugged into a Marshall JTM-45 amp and 4x12 cabinet (with EVs) for the track. He engaged the instrument's "out-of-phase" wiring option to produce the remarkably hollow, nasal tone (sort of a bizarre cross between Billy Gibbons's raunch, a stuck wah-wah, and a clavinet) with its unusual harmonics and reso-nance; which so perfectly complements the plucked rhythm-guitar attack and the sarcas-tic bent of the tune.

"Money for Nothing" is a showcase for Knopfler's claw-style, rhythm/lead finger-picking technique—applied to an eighties rock context. In the main riff and verses, his approach is decidedly "Stones-ish," with simple, mostly two-note power chords finger-plucked à la Ry Cooder or Keith Richards—reflecting a marriage of country blues and hard rock/power-pop guitar styles. With the staccato plucking approach and the out-of-phase sound, Mark creates a memorable rhythm-guitar figure and groove decorated with quirky tonal nuance—quite different from the typical strummed power chords of most hard rock fare.

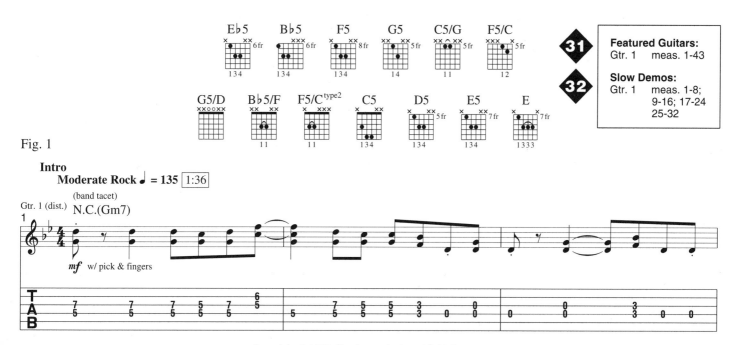

WALK OF LIFE
(Brothers in Arms – 1985)

Words and Music by Mark Knopfler

Fig. 1 – Intro and Main Riff

Another gigantic hit from the *Brothers in Arms* album, "Walk of Life" reached #7 on the charts and held that position for fifteen weeks in late 1985 and early 1986. "Walk of Life" is a case of "rockabilly meets techno pop," and provides us with another example of Mark Knopfler's eclectic composing and arranging approach. Here, the seemingly unlikely mixture yields a beautiful result as he weds vintage-rock guitar sounds to layered keyboard lines over an infectious, zydeco-influenced groove. Acoustic and electric guitars are found in this tune and the blend is epitomized in the intro. Ringing open chords and barre chords on steel-string acoustic (Gtr. 1) dominate the opening measures (9–16). Mark's fat but stinging Tele (Gtr. 2) enters at 0:35 with a classic "picking rhythm" texture and technique which has its roots in the styles of Carl Perkins, Scotty Moore, and James Burton. The sound is appropriately semi-clean and twangy, lightly palm-muted, and colored with a tight slap-back echo effect which enhances the grooving, boogie woogie bass-lines and partial-chord patterns of the guitar part. Note the use of only the I, IV, and V chords (E, A, and B) in the progression—another indication of the "roots-of-rock" conception which is at the heart of this piece.

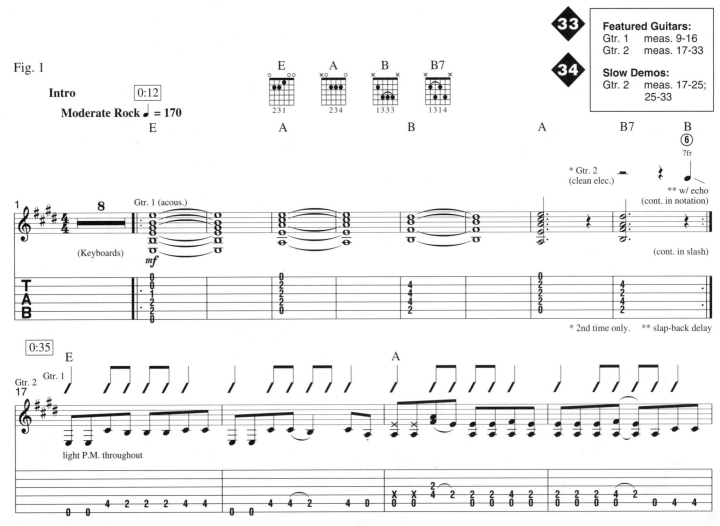

BROTHERS IN ARMS
(Brothers in Arms – 1985)

Words and Music by Mark Knopfler

Fig. 1 – Guitar Solo 1

The title track from the *Brothers in Arms* album is a moody and majestic Knopfler anti-war statement decorated with haunting guitar work. Mark adopts a rich, full-bodied sound and a relaxed, melodic phrasing reminiscent of jazz saxophone throughout the piece, and again showcases his new-found distorted Les Paul tone—this time employing its sustain and density to good advantage. His first solo occurs at 3:36, and is played in the song's G♯ minor modal center. It is a brief (ten-measure) but moving section featuring smoldering single-note lines and strong, well-placed thematic ideas. Notice the trademark Knopfler melodic trait of building melodies from arpeggios of the underlying chords. In the first phrase, a pure G♯m7 (G♯–B–D♯–F♯) arpeggio is played over G♯m–E and is resolved to an E note (the third of C♯m and the root of E) for the C♯m–E changes of measure 2. This sort of tight melodic structure is strictly intuitive on Mark's part, yet it is at the core of his style and characterizes much of his single-note improvisation. Regarding thematic development, check out the many recurrences and elaborations of the opening G♯ minor arpeggio idea during this solo. Also noteworthy in the solo is Knopfler's feel for rhythmic placement of the melodies. His lines have a soulful, story-telling quality and an inevitability associated with blues improvisation—even in this very "non-blues" context. It is this attribute which has distinguished the work of the most innovative blues/rock guitar soloists of history—Santana, Clapton, Hendrix, and Knopfler.

* Audio begins 1 measure before Fig. 1.

** Chords implied by keybds. & bass.

*played behind the beat   *swell-in w/ vol. pedal

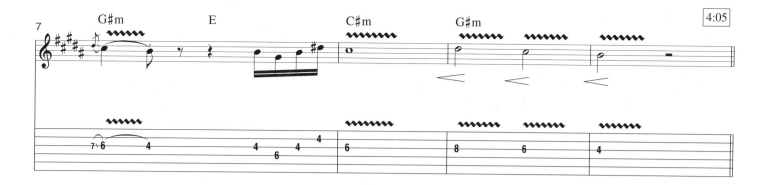

Fig. 2 – Outro Guitar Solo

Mark's outro solo at 4:50 is no less impressive, growing organically out of the ideas, feel, and themes introduced earlier. Notice the allusions to previous material in the distinct G# minor and G#m7 arpeggio lines of measures 1 and 9 which are clearly related to his earlier melodies—as are the smooth sax-like phrasing and thick woody tone of the guitar. This is a more extended outing and Knopfler stretches out with numerous new ideas and textures. These include the double stops with common tones (which produce a secondary thematic idea—that of dyad texture, in this solo) found in measures 5 and 17, as well as the longer, more intricate diatonic scalar lines in measures 3, 4, and 13.

36	Featured Guitars: Gtr. 1 meas. 1-21
37	Slow Demos: Gtr. 1 meas. 1-8; 9-21

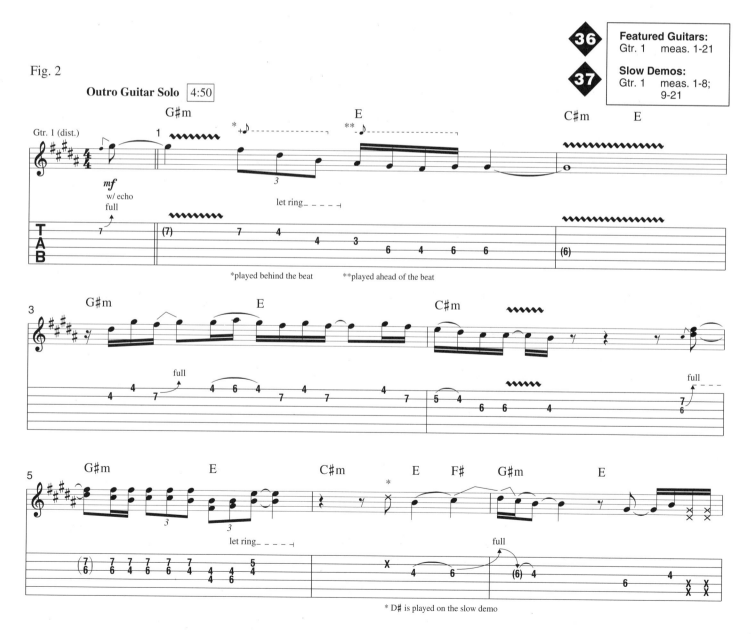

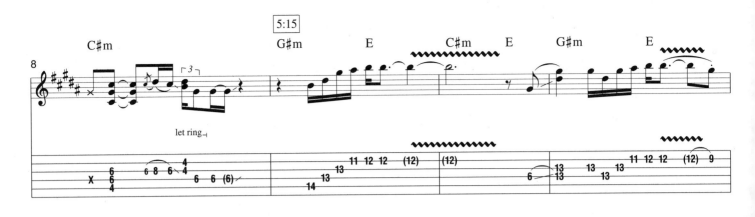

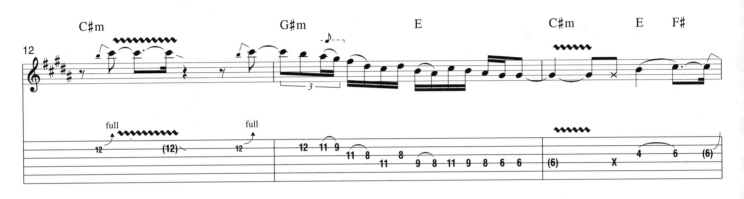

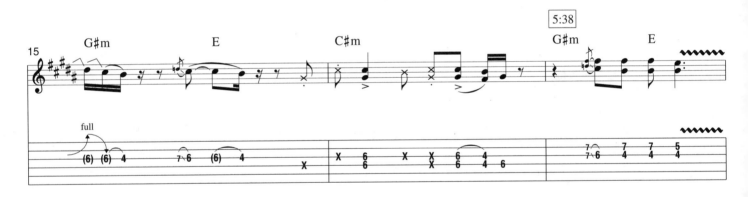

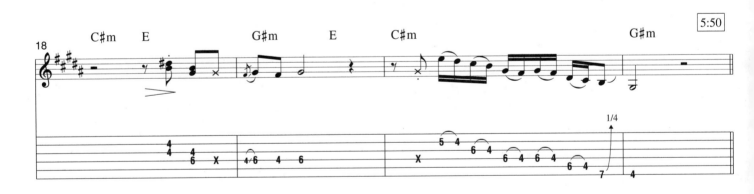

YOU AND YOUR FRIEND
(On Every Street – 1991)

Words and Music by Mark Knopfler

Fig. 1 – Intro

The unusual sound which begins this atmospheric Dire Straits track comes to us courtesy of guitarist Paul Franklin. Franklin is a phenomenal steel player who hooked up with Mark Knopfler and company in the early nineties and contributed much to the guitar interplay of 1991's *On Every Street,* the band's first new album in over six years. "You and Your Friend" affords us an excellent opportunity to examine this interplay. The opening riff, heard twice in the first eight measures and elsewhere in the song, is a gutsy country/blues line rendered on lap steel. This style involves playing a metal-body, resonator-type acoustic guitar (such as the National, so prized by Knopfler), generally in an open tuning and inverted on your lap, using a slide bar (not a metal tube or bottleneck) for the slides, Hawaiian style. The riff makes use of open C6 tuning, a classic country and Hawaiian slack tuning (slack means lowering the strings' pitches). To produce this tuning, begin by dropping your sixth string (E) two whole steps to C and the fourth string (D) a whole step to C. The third string (G) is lowered one-and-a-half steps to E, the second string (B) is dropped two whole steps to G and the first string (E) is lowered a fifth (seven half steps!) to A. The fifth string A is the only pitch to remain in standard tuning. This results in an open-string layout of (from low to high): C–A–C–E–G–A, a C major sixth chord. In "You and Your Friend," the C6 tuning is adapted to create lines in C minor.

As a wonderful sonic complement, Knopfler harnesses his out-of-phase Les Paul tone (see "Money for Nothing"), colored with subtle echo repeats, for the throaty lead lines which dominate the intro (from 0:20–1:02). He plays flowing and expressive blues melodies over the recurring Gm–Bb–G/B–Cm–Ab–Gm progression, which not only kick off the tune in grand style but foreshadow the beautiful guitar work in the outro. Mark's lines are largely in G minor pentatonic (G–Bb–C–D–F) and the G blues scale (G–Bb–C–Db–D–F) for the Gm–Bb–G/B portions of the progression, and in C minor hexatonic (C–D–Eb–F–G–Bb) for the Cm–Ab changes. Notice how he works the third position blues box shape (minor pentatonic pattern 1) to accommodate both standard G minor pentatonic melodies and not-so-standard C minor hexatonic lines.

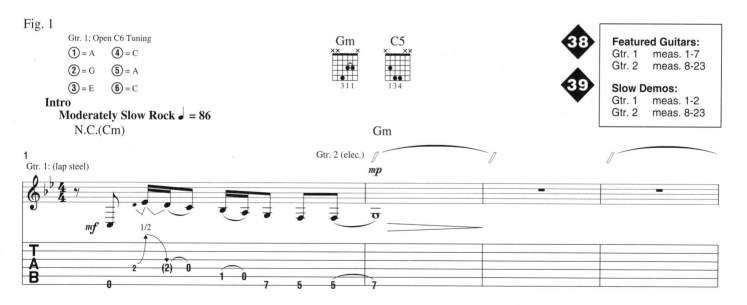

Fig. 1

Fig. 2 – Outro Guitar Solo

Guitar interplay is the name of the game in the outro solo. This extended section (two minutes plus) affords both Knopfler and Franklin an excellent opportunity to stretch out and create memorable melodic solos over a repeating eight-measure vamp (chorus). It starts at 3:32 with Mark doling out sinuous, bluesy lines on electric guitar which are deeper elaborations of his opening ideas. He takes two choruses of eight measures and then passes it over to Paul for two more at 4:15—who rises to the occasion with a sultry and singable statement skillfully combining country, Delta blues, and Hawaiian tangents. From 4:59 to 5:21 (fifth chorus), both players weave restrained lines around each other for eight measures with Knopfler's phrases taking the lead by the middle of the chorus and Franklin's terse fill melodies providing a sympathetic contrapuntal accompaniment. The final full chorus from 5:21 to 5:43 is a smoldering rideout statement showcasing Mark's exciting electric style. Throughout all five choruses, Franklin's rootsy acoustic sound and approach acts as the perfect foil for Knopfler's sophisticated, smoothly-distorted blues-rock lines—together yielding one of the most compelling and gorgeous guitar moments in the Dire Straits catalog.

Featured Guitars:
Gtr. 2   meas. 1-16
Gtr. 1   meas. 17-32
Gtr. 2   meas. 23-25;
          32-49

Slow Demos:
Gtr. 2   meas. 1-17
Gtr. 1   meas. 17-32
Gtr. 2   meas. 23-25;
          32-49

Fig. 2

Outro Guitar Solo 3:32

* Played ahead of the beat.
** Played behind the beat.

55

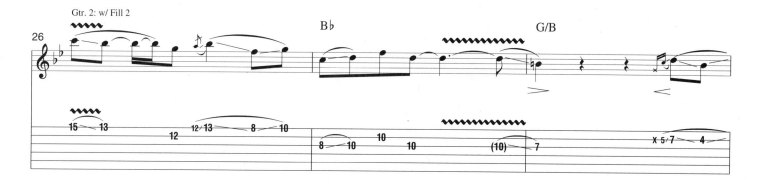

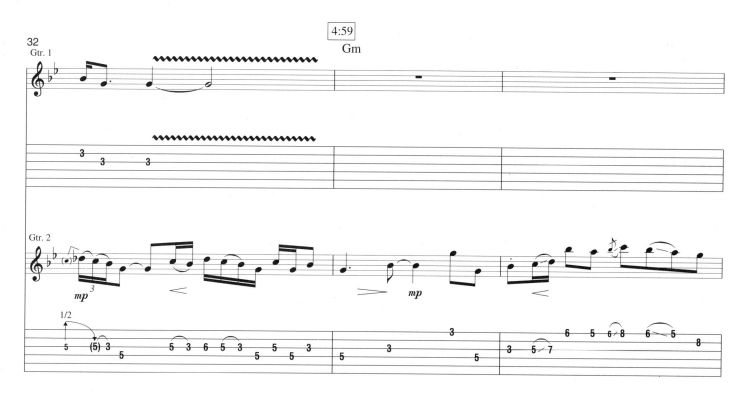

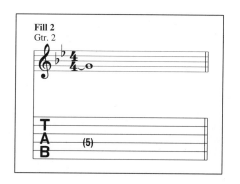

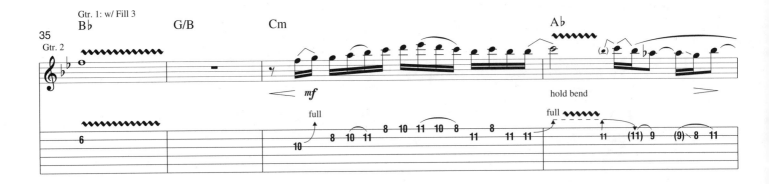

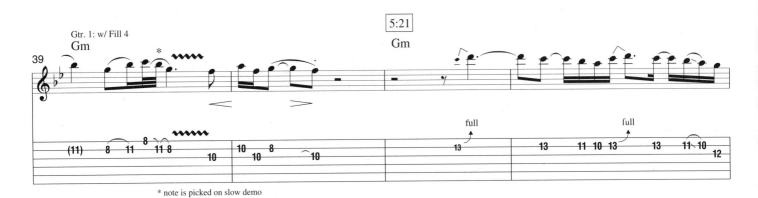

* note is picked on slow demo

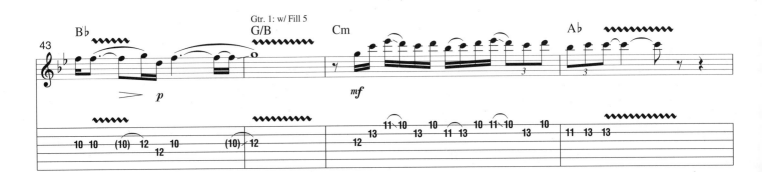

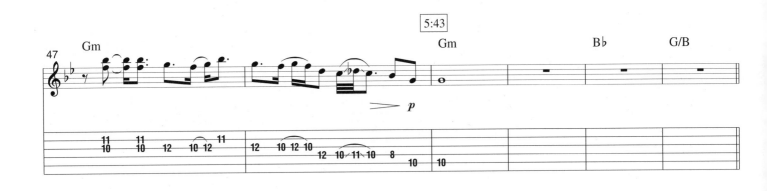

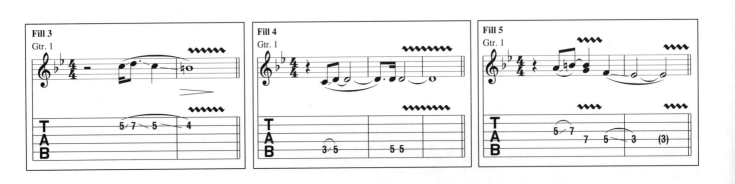

HEAVY FUEL
(On Every Street – 1991)
Words and Music by Mark Knopfler

Fig. 1 – Intro, Verse, and Chorus

"Heavy Fuel" is modern hard rock, Knopfler style, and that's saying a lot. A stand-out favorite from *On Every Street,* this bruiser is distinguished by thick distorted guitar tones, a crushing power riff, and heavy metallic chording which reveals another side to the man—that of an unabashed rocker. Appropriately, it features Mark's new "fat Strat" (a custom-made Pensa-Suhr model) sound through a 100-watt Soldano amp—his primary rock guitar voice of the nineties to the present.

The intro gets right down to it with huge ringing power chords and funky dyad riffs to set up a heavy main rhythm riff in E. The shapes here are reminiscent of the partial-chord approach used on "Money For Nothing," but played with more of an edge. Note the familiar pull-off figure in the pattern (E5 to E4 dyads) in measures 2, 4, 6, and 8. In measures 9–16 (0:15), Mark gives Led Zeppelin a run for their money with a grinding, largely single-note, riff in E. This figure uses notes from the E minor pentatonic (E–G–A–B–D) and E blues (E–G–A–B♭–B–D) scales as well as E5 power chord outlines in its melody. It appears again as a strong secondary riff between the chorus and verse. At 0:24, the verse calms down slightly and Knopfler creates a suitable guitar part made of muted E5 dyads in a grooving eighth-note rhythm with strong rhythmic accents. He uses a technique of muting selectively (lifting off with the fret hand and palm muting) to allow certain accents in the figure (such as beats 1, the "and" of 2, and 4 in measures 3, 5, and 7) to be heard as definite chords while the rest of the plucked shapes remain sheer percussive textures or incidental harmonic clusters. The chorus at 0:44 is ultra-heavy with crunchy power chords, again embellished with that trademark pull-off dyad figure, spelling out the rising C5–D5–E5 progression.

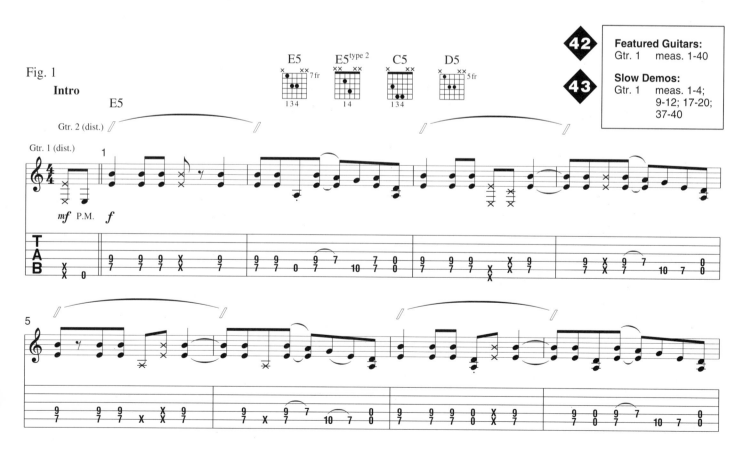

Featured Guitars:
Gtr. 1   meas. 1-40

Slow Demos:
Gtr. 1   meas. 1-4;
9-12; 17-20;
37-40

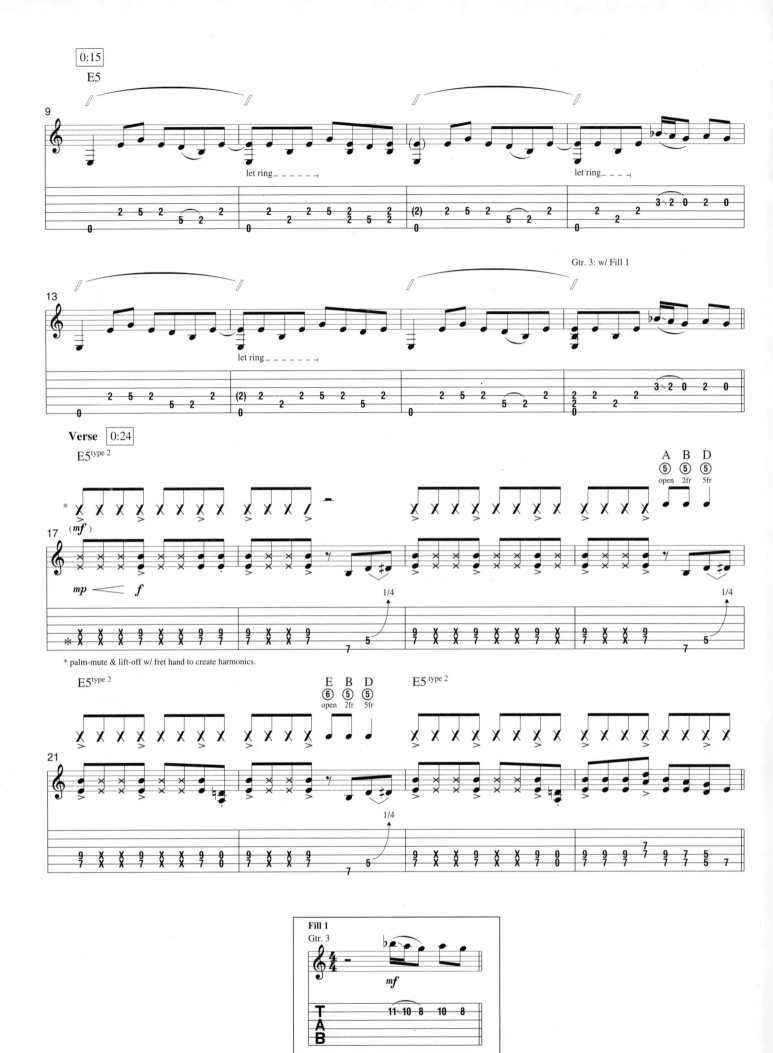

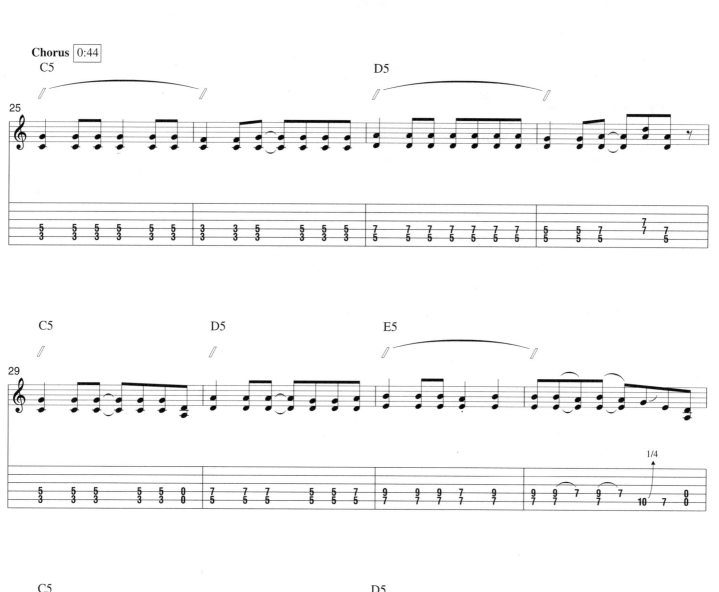

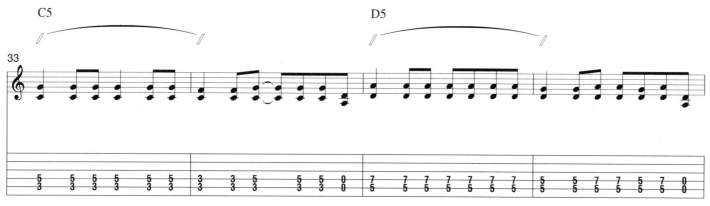

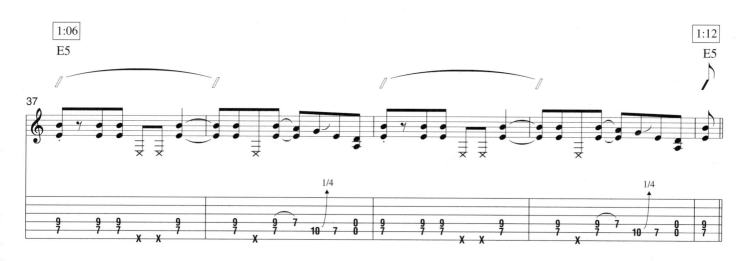

PLANET OF NEW ORLEANS
(On Every Street – 1991)

Words and Music by Mark Knopfler

Fig. 1 – Intro

Among the many styles explored by Mark Knopfler and Dire Straits, modern jazz is one of the most elusive to pin down. Hinted at in various runs, harmonic gestures, and rhythmic phrases in their repertoire, it was overtly pursued in "Planet of New Orleans" from *On Every Street.* This dramatic piece begins gently with a spellbinding *rubato* (free time) intro played by electric guitar with light keyboard accompaniment. Here, Mark evokes the spirit and intent of jazz saxophone with a thick woody tone (via his Pensa-Suhr Strat and the overdriven Soldano SLO-100), breathy delivery, and gorgeous elastic phrasing—laying down simple melodies which weave through the sophisticated backing changes with the ease and grace of a master wind player. Check out the vocalesque volume pedal lines (reminiscent of Larry Carlton's fusion guitar approach) in measures 5–6 and 11–12, as well as the frequent use of color tones, chromaticism (as in measures 3 and 8), and upper harmonic extensions (sevenths, ninths and elevenths) in Knopfler's melodies. These elements foreshadow the strong jazz implications to follow in the body of the tune.

Featured Guitars:
Gtr. 1   meas. 1-20

Slow Demos:
(none)

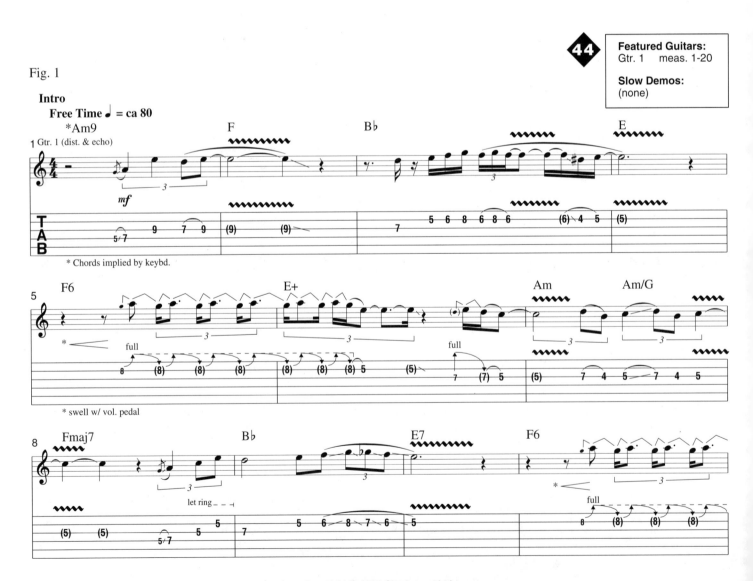

Fig. 1

Intro

Free Time ♩ = ca 80

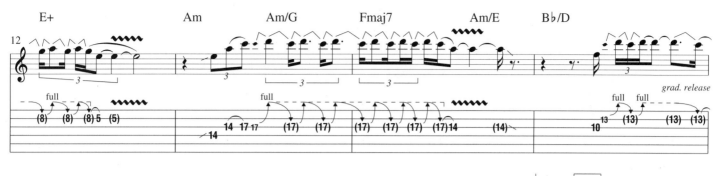

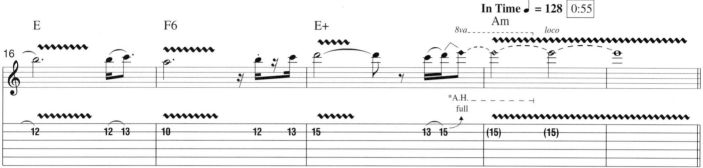

*A.H. (artificial harmonic) produced by touching str. w/ fingertip.

Fig. 2 – Guitar Solo

Mark's first solo at 4:01 is succinct and expositional. He introduces basic themes and concepts to be developed later. These include the particular half-step bend motive (B–C) which emphasizes the tonic minor ninth of the A minor key center (Am9) in measures 1–3 and 9–12, as well as the expressive blues and minor pentatonic lines in measures 5–8 and 13–16. The combined phrases strike an artful balance of jazz and blues melody—of sophistication and soul. Again Knopfler favors a sax-like legato approach (epitomized in the bends and slurs of his phrasing) and robust sustaining tone. A second guitar (Gtr. 2) provides some light funky comping with a contrastingly clean and sparkling Strat sound.

Featured Guitars:
Gtr. 1   meas. 1-18

Slow Demos:
Gtr. 1   meas. 1-18

Fig. 2

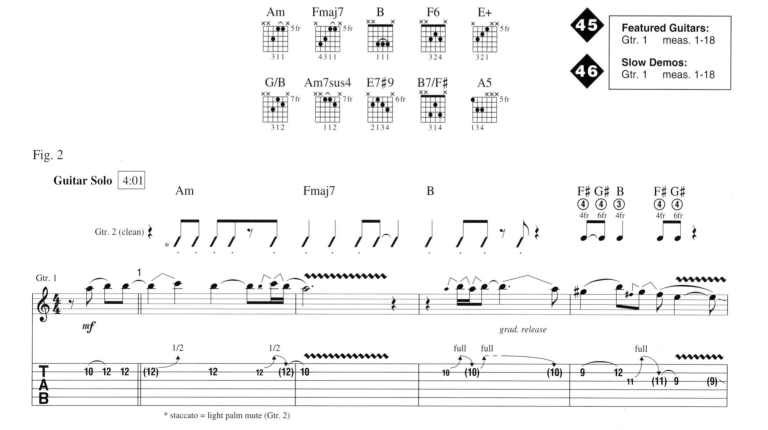

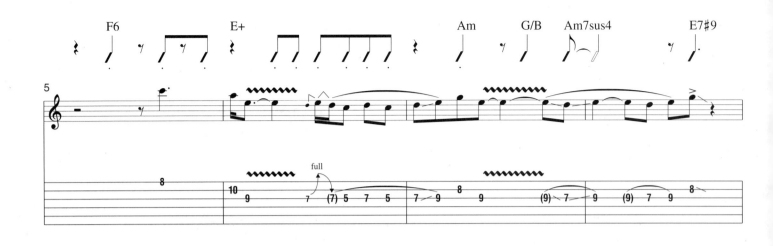

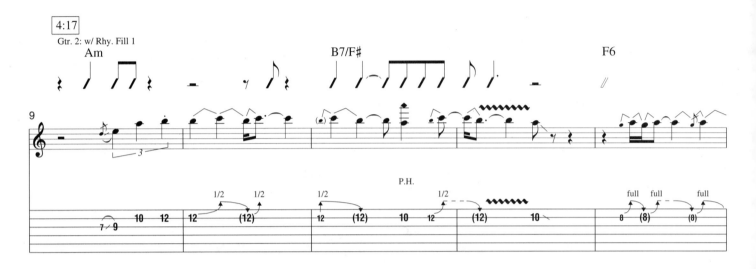

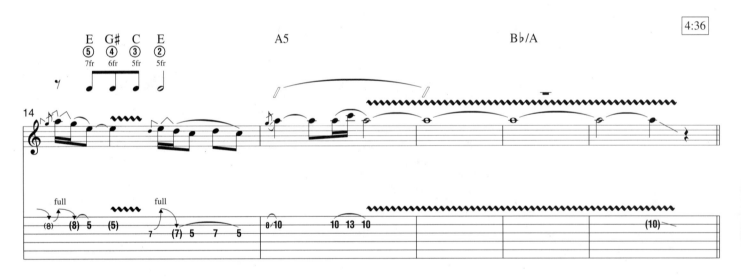

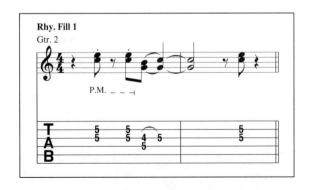

Fig. 3 – Outro Guitar Solo

Knopfler's four-and-a-half chorus outro solo from 6:55 to the fade-out is more extended. The repeating six-measure progression of Am–F–B♭–E7–F6–E+ is definitive and combines—in one nuclear set of changes—his penchant for "Spanish-flamenco" and "European" tonalities, minor blues modality, and jazz harmony. Improvisationally, it is a superb showcase for Mark's melodic guitar inventions. Again he milks sultry string bends throughout, leaning heavily on crying bend-and-release motives in measures 6, 9, 11, 18, 21, and 23 as an elaboration of themes presented in the first solo. His solo lines are again drawn largely from A minor pentatonic (A–C–D–E–G) as an overall scale source, but each chord of the progression is approached individually with great concern for its melodic effect. This is particularly evident in the tight resolution to the B note of the E7 chord in measures 4, 10, and 16 of the first three choruses. Knopfler builds his solo with a strong sense of motion, direction, and logic. The movement toward the two climaxes at 7:17 and 7:28, the third and fourth choruses respectively, is inescapable. The first climax is a gutsy passage of slurred double stops followed by an aggressive blues pull-off lick. The second is a blistering double-timed run of rapid sixteenth-note blues lines reminiscent of the florid blowing of a jazz saxophone.

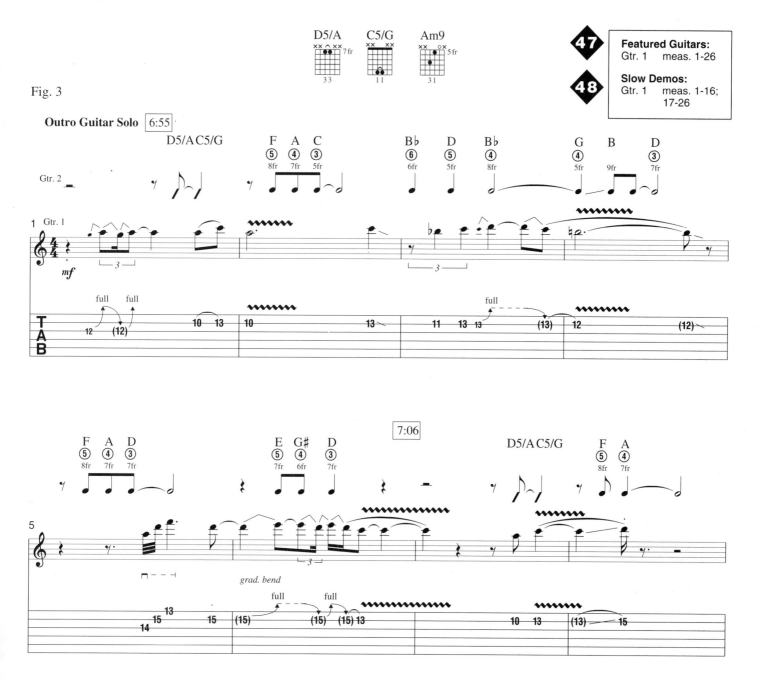

Featured Guitars:
Gtr. 1   meas. 1-26

Slow Demos:
Gtr. 1   meas. 1-16;
          17-26

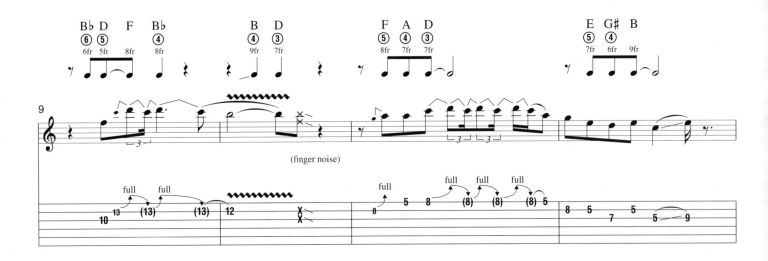

(finger noise)

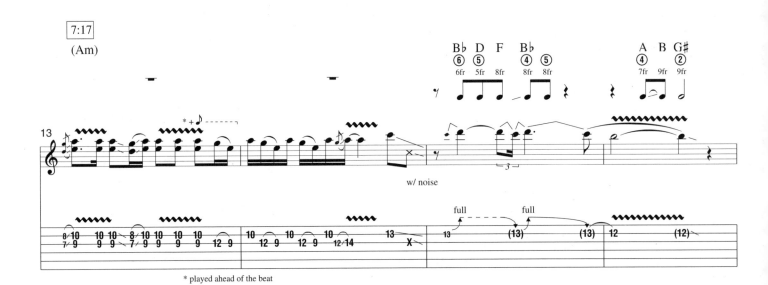

* played ahead of the beat

* played ahead of the beat

w/ noise

*rapid 1/2 step bending.

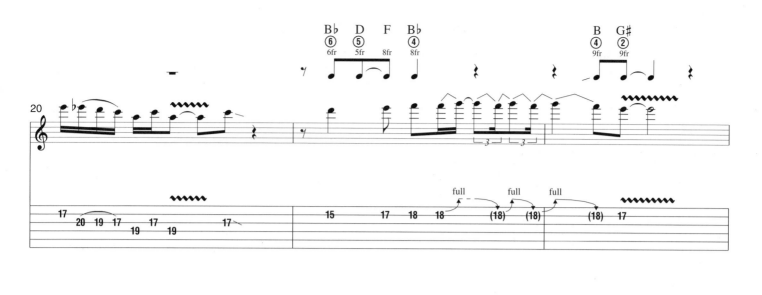

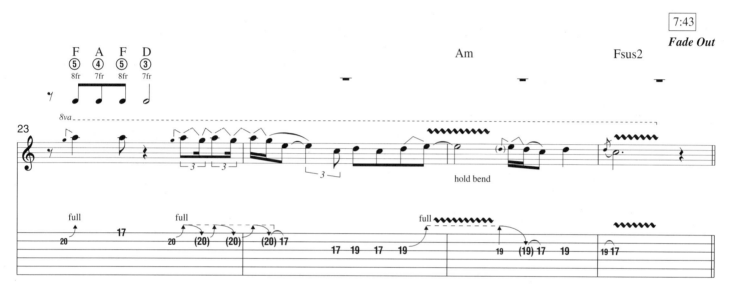

Guitar Notation Legend

Guitar Music can be notated three different ways: on a *musical staff*, in *tablature*, and in *rhythm slashes*.

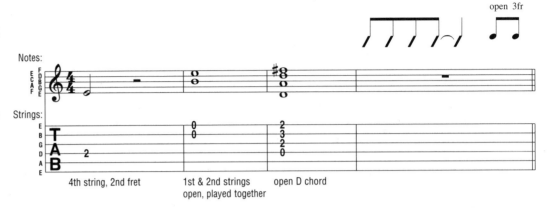

RHYTHM SLASHES are written above the staff. Strum chords in the rhythm indicated. Use the chord diagrams found at the top of the first page of the transcription for the appropriate chord voicings. Round noteheads indicate single notes.

THE MUSICAL STAFF shows pitches and rhythms and is divided by bar lines into measures. Pitches are named after the first seven letters of the alphabet.

TABLATURE graphically represents the guitar fingerboard. Each horizontal line represents a a string, and each number represents a fret.

4th string, 2nd fret

1st & 2nd strings open, played together

open D chord

Definitions for Special Guitar Notation

HALF-STEP BEND: Strike the note and bend up 1/2 step.

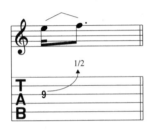

BEND AND RELEASE: Strike the note and bend up as indicated, then release back to the original note. Only the first note is struck.

VIBRATO: The string is vibrated by rapidly bending and releasing the note with the fretting hand.

LEGATO SLIDE: Strike the first note and then slide the same fret-hand finger up or down to the second note. The second note is not struck.

WHOLE-STEP BEND: Strike the note and bend up one step.

PRE-BEND: Bend the note as indicated, then strike it.

WIDE VIBRATO: The pitch is varied to a greater degree by vibrating with the fretting hand.

SHIFT SLIDE: Same as legato slide, except the second note is struck.

GRACE NOTE BEND: Strike the note and bend up as indicated. The first note does not take up any time.

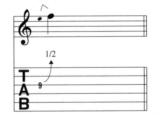

PRE-BEND AND RELEASE: Bend the note as indicated. Strike it and release the bend back to the original note.

HAMMER-ON: Strike the first (lower) note with one finger, then sound the higher note (on the same string) with another finger by fretting it without picking.

TRILL: Very rapidly alternate between the notes indicated by continuously hammering on and pulling off.

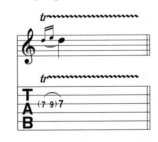

SLIGHT (MICROTONE) BEND: Strike the note and bend up 1/4 step.

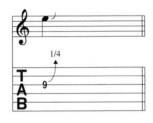

UNISON BEND: Strike the two notes simultaneously and bend the lower note up to the pitch of the higher.

PULL-OFF: Place both fingers on the notes to be sounded. Strike the first note and without picking, pull the finger off to sound the second (lower) note.

TAPPING: Hammer ("tap") the fret indicated with the pick-hand index or middle finger and pull off to the note fretted by the fret hand.

NATURAL HARMONIC: Strike the note while the fret-hand lightly touches the string directly over the fret indicated.

PINCH HARMONIC: The note is fretted normally and a harmonic is produced by adding the edge of the thumb or the tip of the index finger of the pick hand to the normal pick attack.

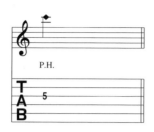

HARP HARMONIC: The note is fretted normally and a harmonic is produced by gently resting the pick hand's index finger directly above the indicated fret (in parentheses) while the pick hand's thumb or pick assists by plucking the appropriate string.

PICK SCRAPE: The edge of the pick is rubbed down (or up) the string, producing a scratchy sound.

MUFFLED STRINGS: A percussive sound is produced by laying the fret hand across the string(s) without depressing, and striking them with the pick hand.

PALM MUTING: The note is partially muted by the pick hand lightly touching the string(s) just before the bridge.

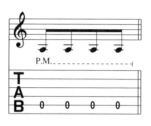

RAKE: Drag the pick across the strings indicated with a single motion.

TREMOLO PICKING: The note is picked as rapidly and continuously as possible.

ARPEGGIATE: Play the notes of the chord indicated by quickly rolling them from bottom to top.

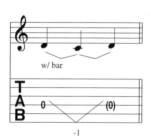

VIBRATO BAR DIVE AND RETURN: The pitch of the note or chord is dropped a specified number of steps (in rhythm) then returned to the original pitch.

VIBRATO BAR SCOOP: Depress the bar just before striking the note, then quickly release the bar.

VIBRATO BAR DIP: Strike the note and then immediately drop a specified number of steps, then release back to the original pitch.

Additional Musical Definitions

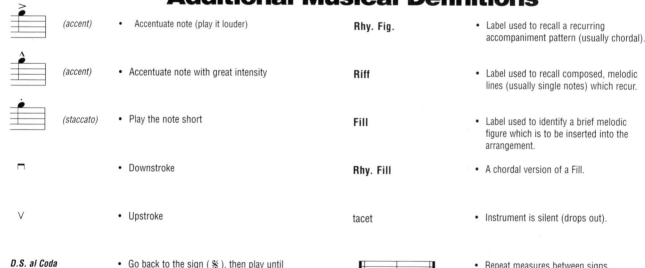

(accent)	•	Accentuate note (play it louder)
(accent)	•	Accentuate note with great intensity
(staccato)	•	Play the note short
⊓	•	Downstroke
∨	•	Upstroke

D.S. al Coda • Go back to the sign (𝄋), then play until the measure marked "*To Coda*," then skip to the section labelled "*Coda*."

D.S. al Fine • Go back to the beginning of the song and play until the measure marked "*Fine*" (end).

Rhy. Fig. • Label used to recall a recurring accompaniment pattern (usually chordal).

Riff • Label used to recall composed, melodic lines (usually single notes) which recur.

Fill • Label used to identify a brief melodic figure which is to be inserted into the arrangement.

Rhy. Fill • A chordal version of a Fill.

tacet • Instrument is silent (drops out).

• Repeat measures between signs.

• When a repeated section has different endings, play the first ending only the first time and the second ending only the second time.

NOTE: Tablature numbers in parentheses mean:
1. The note is being sustained over a system (note in standard notation is tied), or
2. The note is sustained, but a new articulation (such as a hammer-on, pull-off, slide or vibrato begins, or
3. The note is a barely audible "ghost" note (note in standard notation is also in parentheses).

GUITAR *signature licks*

The Signature Licks book/audio packs are especially formatted to give guitarists instruction on how to play a particular artist style by using the actual transcribed, "right from the record" licks! Designed for use by anyone from beginner right up to the experienced player who is looking to expand their insight. The books contain full performance notes and an overview of each artist or group's style with transcriptions in notes and tab. The audio features full-demo playing tips and techniques, as well as playing examples at a slower tempo.

ACOUSTIC GUITAR OF '60S AND '70S
by Wolf Marshall
00695024 Book/CD Pack $19.95

ACOUSTIC GUITAR OF '80S AND '90S
by Wolf Marshall
00695033 Book/CD Pack $19.95

AEROSMITH 1973-1979
by Wolf Marshall
00695106 Book/CD Pack $19.95

AEROSMITH 1979-1998
by Wolf Marshall
00695219 Book/CD Pack $19.95

BEATLES BASS
by Wolf Marshall
00695283 Book/CD Pack $17.95

THE BEATLES FAVORITES
by Wolf Marshall
00695096 Book/CD Pack $19.95

THE BEATLES HITS
by Wolf Marshall
00695049 Book/CD Pack $19.95

THE BEST OF BLACK SABBATH
by Troy Stetina
00695249 Book/CD Pack $19.95

BLUES GUITAR CLASSICS
by Wolf Marshall
00695177 Book/CD Pack $17.95

THE BEST OF ERIC CLAPTON
by Jeff Perrin
00695038 Book/CD Pack $19.95

ERIC CLAPTON – THE BLUESMAN
by Andy Aledort
00695040 Book/CD Pack $19.95

ERIC CLAPTON – FROM THE ALBUM UNPLUGGED
by Wolf Marshall
00695250 Book/CD Pack $19.95

THE BEST OF CREAM
by Wolf Marshall
00695251 Book/CD Pack $19.95

THE BEST OF DEF LEPPARD
by Jeff Perrin
00696516 Book/CD Pack $19.95

GREATEST GUITAR SOLOS OF ALL TIME
by Wolf Marshall
00695301 Book/CD Pack $17.95

GUITAR INSTRUMENTAL HITS
by Wolf Marshall
00695309 Book/CD Pack $16.95

GUITAR RIFFS OF THE '60S
by Wolf Marshall
00695218 Book/CD pack $16.95

GUITAR RIFFS OF THE '70S
by Wolf Marshall
00695158 Book/CD Pack $16.95

THE BEST OF GUNS N' ROSES
by Jeff Perrin
00695183 Book/CD Pack $19.95

JIMI HENDRIX
by Andy Aledort
00696560 Book/CD Pack $19.95

ERIC JOHNSON
by Wolf Marshall
00699317 Book/CD Pack $19.95

THE BEST OF KISS
by Jeff Perrin
00699413 Book/CD Pack $19.95

MARK KNOPFLER
by Wolf Marshall
00695178 Book/CD Pack $19.95

MEGADETH
by Jeff Perrin
00695041 Book/CD Pack $19.95

THE GUITARS OF ELVIS
by Wolf Marshall
00696507 Book/CD Pack $19.95

BEST OF QUEEN
by Wolf Marshall
00695097 Book/CD Pack $19.95

THE RED HOT CHILI PEPPERS
by Dale Turner
00695173 Book/CD Pack $19.95

THE ROLLING STONES
by Wolf Marshall
00695079 Book/CD Pack $19.95

BEST OF CARLOS SANTANA
by Wolf Marshall
00695010 Book/CD Pack $19.95

THE BEST OF JOE SATRIANI
by Dale Turner
00695216 Book/CD Pack $19.95

STEVE VAI
by Jeff Perrin
00673247 Book/CD Pack $22.95

STEVE VAI – ALIEN LOVE SECRETS: THE NAKED VAMPS
00695223 Book/CD Pack $19.95

STEVE VAI – FIRE GARDEN: THE NAKED VAMPS
00695166 Book/CD Pack $19.95

STEVIE RAY VAUGHAN
by Wolf Marshall
00699316 Book/CD Pack $19.95

THE GUITAR STYLE OF STEVIE RAY VAUGHAN
by Wolf Marshall
00695155 Book/CD Pack $19.95

FOR MORE INFORMATION, SEE YOUR LOCAL MUSIC DEALER,
OR WRITE TO:

HAL•LEONARD® CORPORATION

7777 W. BLUEMOUND RD. P.O. BOX 13819 MILWAUKEE, WI 53213

Prices, contents and availability subject to change without notice.

0199

RECORDED VERSIONS
The Best Note-For-Note Transcriptions Available

ALL BOOKS INCLUDE TABLATURE

90199 Aerosmith – Nine Lives $19.95	00690068 Return Of The Hellecasters $19.95	00690090 Red Hot Chili Peppers – One Hot Minute .$22.95
90146 Aerosmith – Toys in the Attic $19.95	00692930 Jimi Hendrix – Are You Experienced? . .$24.95	00694892 Guitar Style Of Jerry Reed $19.95
94865 Alice In Chains – Dirt $19.95	00692931 Jimi Hendrix – Axis: Bold As Love $22.95	00694937 Jimmy Reed – Master Bluesman $19.95
94932 Allman Brothers Band – Volume 1 . . . . .$24.95	00692932 Jimi Hendrix – Electric Ladyland $24.95	00694899 R.E.M. – Automatic For The People $19.95
94933 Allman Brothers Band – Volume 2 . . . . .$24.95	00690218 Jimi Hendrix – First Rays of the New Rising Sun $24.95	00690260 Jimmie Rodgers Guitar Collection $17.95
94934 Allman Brothers Band – Volume 3 . . . . .$24.95	00690038 Gary Hoey – Best Of $19.95	00690014 Rolling Stones – Exile On Main Street . .$24.95
94877 Chet Atkins – Guitars For All Seasons . . .$19.95	00660029 Buddy Holly $19.95	00690186 Rolling Stones – Rock & Roll Circus . . .$19.95
94918 Randy Bachman Collection $22.95	00660169 John Lee Hooker – A Blues Legend $19.95	00690135 Otis Rush Collection $19.95
94880 Beatles – Abbey Road $19.95	00690054 Hootie & The Blowfish –	00690031 Santana's Greatest Hits $19.95
94863 Beatles –	Cracked Rear View $19.95	00694805 Scorpions – Crazy World $19.95
Sgt. Pepper's Lonely Hearts Club Band . .$19.95	00694905 Howlin' Wolf $19.95	00690150 Son Seals – Bad Axe Blues $17.95
90174 Beck – Mellow Gold $17.95	00690136 Indigo Girls – 1200 Curfews $22.95	00690128 Seven Mary Three – American Standards .$19.95
90346 Beck – Mutations $19.95	00694938 Elmore James –	00690076 Sex Pistols – Never Mind The Bollocks .$19.95
90175 Beck – Odelay $17.95	Master Electric Slide Guitar $19.95	00120105 Kenny Wayne Shepherd – Ledbetter Heights $19.95
94884 The Best of George Benson $19.95	00690167 Skip James Blues Guitar Collection . . .$16.95	00120123 Kenny Wayne Shepherd – Trouble Is . . .$19.95
92385 Chuck Berry $19.95	00694833 Billy Joel For Guitar $19.95	00690196 Silverchair – Freak Show $19.95
92200 Black Sabbath –	00694912 Eric Johnson – Ah Via Musicom $19.95	00690130 Silverchair – Frogstomp $19.95
We Sold Our Soul For Rock 'N' Roll . .$19.95	00690169 Eric Johnson – Venus Isle $22.95	00690041 Smithereens – Best Of $19.95
90115 Blind Melon – Soup $19.95	00694799 Robert Johnson – At The Crossroads . . .$19.95	00694885 Spin Doctors – Pocket Full Of Kryptonite $19.95
90305 Blink 182 – Dude Ranch $19.95	00693185 Judas Priest – Vintage Hits $19.95	00690124 Sponge – Rotting Pinata $19.95
90241 Bloodhound Gang – One Fierce Beer Coaster .$19.95	00690277 Best of Kansas $19.95	00120004 Steely Dan – Best Of $24.95
90028 Blue Oyster Cult – Cult Classics $19.95	00690073 B. B. King – 1950-1957 . . . .$24.95	00694921 Steppenwolf, The Best Of $22.95
90219 Blur $19.95	00690098 B. B. King – 1958-1967 . . . .$24.95	00694957 Rod Stewart – Acoustic Live $22.95
94935 Boston: Double Shot Of $22.95	00690099 B. B. King – 1962-1971 . . . .$24.95	00690021 Sting – Fields Of Gold $19.95
90237 Meredith Brooks – Blurring the Edges . . .$19.95	00690134 Freddie King Collection $17.95	00120081 Sublime $19.95
90168 Roy Buchanon Collection $19.95	00694903 The Best Of Kiss $24.95	00120122 Sublime – 40 Oz. to Freedom $19.95
90337 Jerry Cantrell – Boggy Depot $19.95	00690157 Kiss – Alive $19.95	00690242 Suede – Coming Up $19.95
90293 Best of Steven Curtis Chapman $19.95	00690163 Mark Knopfler/Chet Atkins – Neck and Neck $19.95	00694824 Best Of James Taylor $16.95
90043 Cheap Trick – Best Of $19.95	00690296 Patty Larkin Songbook $17.95	00694887 Thin Lizzy – The Best Of Thin Lizzy . .$19.95
20151 Best of the Chemical Brothers $14.95	00690202 Live – Secret Samadhi $19.95	00690238 Third Eye Blind $19.95
90171 Chicago – Definitive Guitar Collection $22.95	00690070 Live – Throwing Copper $19.95	00690022 Richard Thompson Guitar $19.95
90139 Eric Clapton – Journeyman $19.95	00690018 Living Colour – Best Of $19.95	00690267 311 . . . .$19.95
94869 Eric Clapton – Live Acoustic $19.95	00694954 Lynyrd Skynyrd, New Best Of $19.95	00690030 Toad The Wet Sprocket $19.95
94896 John Mayall/Eric Clapton – Bluesbreakers $19.95	00694845 Yngwie Malmsteen – Fire And Ice $19.95	00690228 Tonic – Lemon Parade $19.95
90162 Best of the Clash $19.95	00694956 Bob Marley – Legend $19.95	00690295 Tool – Aenima $19.95
90166 Albert Collins – The Alligator Years $16.95	00690283 Best of Sarah McLachlan $19.95	00694411 U2 – The Joshua Tree $19.95
94940 Counting Crows – August & Everything After $19.95	00690239 Matchbox 20 – Yourself or Someone Like You .$19.95	00690039 Steve Vai – Alien Love Secrets $24.95
90197 Counting Crows – Recovering the Satellites .$19.95	00690244 Megadeath – Cryptic Writings $19.95	00690172 Steve Vai – Fire Garden $24.95
90118 Cranberries – The Best of $19.95	00690236 Mighty Mighty Bosstones – Let's Face It . . .$19.95	00690023 Jimmie Vaughan – Strange Pleasures . . .$19.95
90215 Music of Robert Cray $19.95	00690040 Steve Miller Band Greatest Hits $19.95	00660136 Stevie Ray Vaughan – In Step $19.95
94840 Cream – Disraeli Gears $19.95	00690225 Moist – Creature $19.95	00694835 Stevie Ray Vaughan – The Sky Is Crying .$19.95
90007 Danzig 4 . . . .$19.95	00694802 Gary Moore – Still Got The Blues $19.95	00694776 Vaughan Brothers – Family Style $19.95
90184 DC Talk – Jesus Freak $19.95	00690103 Alanis Morissette – Jagged Little Pill . . .$19.95	00690217 Verve Pipe, The – Villains $19.95
90186 Alex De Grassi Guitar Collection $19.95	00690341 Alanis Morisette –	00120026 Joe Walsh – Look What I Did... . . . . .$24.95
90289 Best of Deep Purple $17.95	Supposed Former Infatuation Junkie . . .$19.95	00694789 Muddy Waters – Deep Blues $24.95
94831 Derek And The Dominos –	00694958 Mountain, Best Of $19.95	00690071 Weezer $19.95
Layla & Other Assorted Love Songs $19.95	00694913 Nirvana – In Utero $19.95	00690286 Weezer – Pinkerton $19.95
90322 Ani Di Franco – Little Plastic Castle $19.95	00694883 Nirvana – Nevermind $19.95	00694970 Who, The – Definitive Collection A-E . .$24.95
90187 Dire Straits – Brothers In Arms $19.95	00690026 Nirvana – Acoustic In New York $19.95	00694971 Who, The – Definitive Collection F-Li . .$24.95
90191 Dire Straits – Money For Nothing $24.95	00120112 No Doubt – Tragic Kingdom $22.95	00694972 Who, The – Definitive Collection Lo-R . .$24.95
90178 Willie Dixon – Master Blues Composer . . .$24.95	00690121 Oasis – (What's The Story) Morning Glory .$19.95	00694973 Who, The – Definitive Collection S-Y . .$24.95
90250 Best of Duane Eddy $16.95	00690290 Offspring, The – Ignition $19.95	00690320 Best of Dar Williams $17.95
90323 Fastball – All the Pain Money Can Buy . . .$19.95	00690204 Offspring, The – Ixnay on the Hombre . .$17.95	00690319 Best of Stevie Wonder $19.95
90089 Foo Fighters $19.95	00690203 Offspring, The – Smash $17.95	
90235 Foo Fighters – The Colour and the Shape .$19.95	00694830 Ozzy Osbourne – No More Tears $19.95	
90042 Robben Ford Blues Collection $19.95	00694855 Pearl Jam – Ten $19.95	
94920 Free – Best Of $18.95	00690053 Liz Phair – Whip Smart $19.95	
90324 Fuel – Sunburn $19.95	00690176 Phish – Billy Breathes $22.95	
90222 G3 Live – Satriani, Vai, Johnson $22.95	00690331 Phish – The Story of Ghost $19.95	
94894 Frank Gambale – The Great Explorers . . .$19.95	00693800 Pink Floyd – Early Classics $19.95	
94807 Danny Gatton – 88 Elmira St $19.95	00694967 Police – Message In A Box Boxed Set . . .$70.00	
90127 Goo Goo Dolls – A Boy Named Goo $19.95	00690195 Presidents of the United States of America II $22.95	
90338 Goo Goo Dolls – Dizzy Up the Girl $19.95	00694974 Queen – A Night At The Opera $24.95	
90117 John Gorka Collection $19.95	00690145 Rage Against The Machine – Evil Empire .$19.95	
90114 Buddy Guy Collection Vol. A-J $22.95	00690179 Rancid – And Out Come the Wolves . . .$22.95	
90193 Buddy Guy Collection Vol. L-Y $22.95	00690055 Red Hot Chili Peppers –	
94798 George Harrison Anthology $19.95	Bloodsugarsexmagik $19.95	

Improve Your Groove

ALL BOOKS INCLUDE NOTES & TAB

With Guitar Instruction Book/CD Packs From Hal Leonard!

Classic Rock Guitar Styles
by John Tapella

A complete guide to rhythm and lead guitar in the style of Led Zeppelin, The Who, Eric Clapton, Pink Floyd, The Rolling Stones, Doobie Brothers, The Grateful Dead, and more. Includes lessons on common riffs, progressions, scales, and techniques. The CD includes 25 tracks with music examples, complete pieces, and special jam progressions.

00695042 Book/CD Pack $16.95

Guitar Styles Of The '90s
by John Tapella

Explore guitar in the styles of bands like Pearl Jam, Nirvana, Soundgarden, and Stone Temple Pilots. The CD includes over 20 examples and four complete pieces. Book provides lessons on altered tunings, scales and solo techniques, common chords and rhythms, and more.

00695086 Book/CD Pack . .$14.95

Punk Guitar Method
by John Tapella

"This volume contains all the blistering moves, scales, chords, and rhythm charts you'll ever need..." —*Guitar School*. Take an inside look at the guitar styles of bands like the Sex Pistols, The Ramones, Green Day and The Offspring. Learn common chords, progressions, solo scales and techniques, rhythms and more. CD features 32 musical examples played out and two complete songs.

00695035 Book/CD Pack $17.95

Terrifying Technique For Guitar
by Carl Culpepper

The ultimate source for building chops while improving your technical facility and overcoming physical barriers. Covers: alternate, economy, hybrid, and sweep picking; symmetrical, chromatic, and scale exercises; arpeggios, tapping, legato, and bending sequences – over 200 exercises in all. CD includes full exercise demonstrations.

00695034 Book/CD Pack . .$14.95

Guitarists' Guide To Theory And Harmony
by Jeff Schroedl

This easy-to-follow method teaches how to solo over a chord progression. It covers riffs, blues-based music, extended chords, power chords, major scales and key signatures, triadic and seventh chord harmony, diatonic and non-diatonic progressions, and much more. The CD includes full band backing for reference and play-along.

00695081 Book/CD Pack $14.95

Acoustic Guitar Styles
by John Tapella

Explore guitar in the style of artists like James Taylor, Neil Young, Eric Clapton, Pearl Jam, Oasis, and many others. The book covers strumming and fingerpicking; standard, open, and altered tunings; working with a capo; picking techniques, chord embellishments, home recording, and more! The CD includes over 50 examples and five complete pieces.

00695105 Book/CD Pack . .$14.95

Acoustic Guitar of the '80s and '90s

Learn to play acoustic guitar in the styles and techniques of today's top performers. This book/CD pack features detailed instruction on 15 examples, including: Tears In Heaven • Patience • Losing My Religion • Wanted Dead Or Alive • and more.

00695033 Book/CD Pack $19.95

Blues You Can Use
by John Ganapes

A comprehensive source for learning blues guitar, designed to develop both your lead and rhythm playing. Covers all styles of blues, including Texas, Delta, R&B, early rock and roll, gospel, blues/rock and more. Includes 21 complete solos; blues chords, progressions and riffs; audio with leads and full band backing; and more!

00695007 Book/CD Pack $19.95

Power Trio Blues
by Dave Rubin

This book/CD pack details how to play electric guitar in a trio with bass and drums. Boogie, shuffle, and slow blues rhythms, licks, double stops, chords, and bass patterns are presented for full and exciting blues. A CD with the music examples performed by a smokin' power trio is included for play-along instruction and jamming. The music styles of Chicago and Texas bluesmen are presented along with rare photos of them with their favorite axes.

00695028 Book/CD Pack $19.95

Electric Slide Guitar Method
by David Hamburger

This book/CD pack is a comprehensive examination of slide guitar fundamentals in the styles of Duane Allman, Dave Hole, Ry Cooder, Bonnie Raitt, Muddy Waters, Johnny Winter, and Elmore James. Also includes: sample licks and solos; info on selecting a slide and proper setup; backup/rhythm slide playing; standard and open tunings; and more.

00695022 Book/CD Pack $19.95

The Guitar F/X Cookbook
by Chris Amelar

The ultimate source for guitar tricks, effects, and other unorthodox techniques. This book demonstrates and explains 45 incredible guitar sounds using common stomp boxes and a few unique techniques, including: pick scraping, police siren, ghost slide, church bell, jaw harp, delay swells, looping, monkey's scream, cat's meow, race car, pickup tapping, and much more.

00695080 Book/CD Pack $14.95

Guitar Licks
by Chris Amelar

Learn great licks in the style of players like Clapton, Hendrix, Hammett, Page and more. Includes two complete solos; 40 must-know licks for rock and blues; info on essential techniques; standard notation & tab; and more. CD features demos of every technique, lick and solo in the book

00695141 Book/CD Pack $14.95